PASS YOUR YACHTMASTER

YACHTMASTER

Third Edition

DAVID FAIRHALL • MIKE PEYTON

ADLARD COLES NAUTICAL
London

This edition published 2002 by Adlard Coles Nautical
an imprint of A & C Black Publishers Ltd
37 Soho Square, London W1D 3QZ
www.adlardcoles.com

First edition published by Nautical Books 1982
Reprinted (with corrections) 1983
Reprinted 1986
Second edition 1989
Third edition published by Adlard Coles Nautical 2002

ISBN 0-7136-6259-X

A CIP catalogue record for this book is available from the British Library.

A & C Black uses paper produced with elemental chlorine-free pulp,
harvested from managed sustainable forests.

Typeset in Frutiger
Printed and bound in Great Britain by
The Cromwell Press, Trowbridge, Wiltshire

Note: While all reasonable care has been taken in the publication
of this book, the publisher takes no responsibility for the use of the methods
or products described in the book.

Acknowledgements
The tidal extracts are used with kind permission of The Controller HMSO and the
Hydrographer of the Navy.

Contents

Introduction 1

Navigation 3

Charts • IALA buoyage system • The magnetic compass • The log •
Depth sounding • GPS • Hyperbolic systems • Tides • Chartwork

Weather 37

Weather systems • Clouds • Depressions • Anticyclones • Local weather •
Fog • Beaufort wind scale • Sources of weather information

Safety and seagoing practice 52

Rule of the Road • The International Regulations for Preventing Collisions
at Sea analysed to make learning easier • Communications •
Distress signals • Maritime and Coastguard Agency •
Safety equipment • Stability and buoyancy of yachts • Anchoring •
Coping with bad weather • Passage planning

Index 92

Introduction

The Yachtmaster Offshore course is part of an extensive voluntary training scheme run by the Royal Yachting Association (in co-operation with the Department of Transport) 'to encourage high standards of seamanship and navigation among yachtsmen and women' and avoid unnecessary regulation. Each year thousands of yachtsmen and women attend evening classes as a preparation for the coveted Yachtmaster qualification. This book is unashamedly a 'crammer' for that course – a concise but comprehensive guide to help you revise for (and pass) the assessment examinations.

The RYA prefers not to talk about its shorebased courses as an 'examination process' – it merely awards 'certificates of satisfactory completion'. But whatever you call the exercises and assessment papers, they strike most students as being exams in a format they may not have faced since leaving school. Indeed, some of the exercises have to be taken under invigilation and require detailed knowledge that needs 'swotting up' beforehand. And that is where this book comes in.

We have tried to help by looking for the logic as well as the facts, and eliminating unnecessary information to concentrate on the essentials of the RYA syllabus. In each of the main sections – **navigation, weather, safety and seagoing practice** – we have tried to do four things:

- Provide all the essential information.
- Organise it in a digestible form that makes learning and revision easier – in fact, the book is small enough to slip in your pocket to skim through in the lunch hour, on the train home, or just before going into the exam.
- Advise on exam tactics.
- Set all this in a practical seagoing perspective.

No single textbook is a substitute for the extensive background reading needed, let alone for the instruction itself But we can provide a skeleton, waiting to be fleshed out by teaching, reading and practical experience, because ultimately there is also no substitute for seatime.

'I'll be glad to get in, I've had enough excitement for one day.'

The RYA training scheme operates at five levels – Competent Crew, Day Skipper/Watch Leader, Coastal Skipper, Yachtmaster Offshore, and Yachtmaster Ocean. There are approved courses covering all of these (plus diesel engine maintenance, radar and survival) with practical exams for the last three.

The shorebased course we are concerned with here is a combined one, for **Coastal Skipper/Yachtmaster Offshore** candidates. It involves a minimum of 40 hours teaching plus work at home. The syllabus is set out in RYA pamphlets, for sail and power. To obtain the final qualification, or 'certificate of competence', you must first log 50 days at sea, covering 2500 miles, including at least five 60-mile passages, and also hold a radio operator's certificate and a first aid certificate. The practical exam, for which you need to provide the boat, lasts 8–12 hours, and aims to show that you can competently skipper a cruising yacht up to 150 miles offshore.

We hope this book gets you successfully under way.

To make things easier, we have used bold type and tinted panels to pick out key phrases and facts to help you with your revision.

The symbols at the bottom of each right hand page are to test your knowledge – the answers are overleaf.

Navigation

European navigators first acquired a primitive magnetic compass at least 800 years ago, possibly from China, where the invention was recorded even earlier. Nowadays, courtesy of the US Defense Department, we have navigational satellites to provide a Global Positioning System (GPS) accurate to within a few metres.

But neither of these great technological advances would be much use to us without a chart, to identify our destination and warn of obstacles along the way. Buoys and lighthouses confirming the changing position are also shown on the chart. And, independent of GPS, we also need to be able to measure speed and distance, and find the depth of water. So this section of the book deals with all these sources of navigational information, plus other related subjects covered by the Yachtmaster assessment papers.

The offshore racing yachtsman likes to know precisely where he is at all times. In contrast, those who are cruising often take things a bit easier, provided they anticipate the occasions when they really *do* need an accurate position: winding through sandbanks on a falling tide, for instance, or making landfall in bad visibility. In practice, therefore, navigational techniques range all the way from the crumpled-chart-on-the-cockpit-seat school, right through to the pedantic naval style that expects to have a course plotted from the harbour berth to the pierheads. The would-be Yachtmaster, though, should remember he is still in the classroom preparing for an exam, and so take his cue from the instructor.

The RYA's instructional notes make this same point: 'At sea it is often impracticable or even undesirable to work to high levels of precision, but there are times when the safety of the yacht will depend on precise navigation and accurate calculations. The course exercises assume the latter and the questions require a navigational precision of 0.1 mile and 0.1 metre for tidal calculations.'

Charts

Like land maps, charts are the projection of a curved surface on to a flat sheet of paper. **The common projection is Mercator's**. This spreads out the lines of longitude (measured in degrees east or west of the Greenwich meridian) so that they appear parallel instead of converging at the North Pole, as they do

'I've brought our position up to date, John. Give me a call when we sight land.'

on a globe. But to preserve the shape of the coastline, lines of latitude (measured in degrees from the Equator) also have to spread out as you move north.

An important practical implication of this is that **distances should always be measured along the side of the chart**, where latitude is marked, roughly level with the yacht's position. One minute of latitude – a sixtieth of a degree – is a **nautical mile**, and it averages out (because the earth is not exactly spherical) at 6076 feet or 1852 metres. A **cable** is a tenth of a nautical mile, roughly 200 yards.

On Mercator charts a straight line, or **rhumb line**, is not the shortest distance between two real points. That would be a **great circle**, which appears on the chart as a curved line. In practice, this distortion rarely matters to yachtsmen. However, some charts do show lines of longitude converging as they would on a globe, using a **Gnomonic projection**, so that the shortest distance across an ocean can conveniently be drawn as a straight line.

UK charts

UK charts are drawn from underwater surveys commissioned by the UK Hydrographic Office (UKHO), supplemented by information from similar organisations abroad, and marketed as *Admiralty* charts. This comprehensive series sets the standard. For most parts of the world it is also available in electronic or Raster form. However, these paper charts are primarily designed for

North cardinal buoy

use on the full-sized chart table of a large merchant vessel or warship, so the UKHO has recently produced *Small Craft Folios*, and also folded *Small Craft Editions*, to match those published specifically for yachtsmen by *Imray* and *Stanfords*. Individual sailors will have their own preferences regarding these yachting charts, but they are all suitable for use in a damp cockpit and stuffed into a transparent plastic cover, not just in a sheltered chartroom. The charts also provide lots of supplementary information, selected and presented from the perspective of a small boat rather than a supertanker. Harbour plans and miniature tidal stream charts are particularly useful.

One thing you need to know about any chart is whether it is up to date. Minor changes occur frequently and are often important. It can be extremely disconcerting when a buoy turns up in the 'wrong' position, in a different shape, or simply disappears.

On Admiralty charts, the date of the edition is shown in the margin, plus a reference to the weekly *Notices to Mariners* where relevant corrections are published. Imray give the edition date and attach a list of corrections. Stanfords give the edition and the date to which each chart is corrected. All three publishers can supply further corrections by post and on their respective websites.

Units of depth on charts

The traditional **unit of depth** at sea is the fathom – 6 feet, and some charts, particularly in the USA, still use fathoms. However, nearly all European charts now mark minimum depths in metres and tenths of a metre, so for the purpose of the Yachtmaster course you need only think metric. Where the little numbers scattered across the chart are underlined, this shows the **drying height** above low water.

Symbols

There are thousands of other **symbols and abbreviations**, listed as *Admiralty Chart No 5011* (which is actually a booklet), and many are self-explanatory – like the little drawings of buoys with their various topmarks. Others, such as the symbol for lava flowing down the side of a volcano, can safely be ignored. In any case, this is an area where your instructor will probably allow you to consult sources of reference, unlike when you are sitting the assessment papers on collision regulations, meteorology and chartwork, which must be done under exam conditions.

Many students will be content simply to learn the common symbols as they crop up, but if you do want to do a bit of swotting, some categories are obviously of more importance than others. Ways of marking wrecks and dangerous rocks are one such example, as are the descriptions of light characteristics.

Some commonly used symbols and abbreviations

Wk	wreck
⚓	wreck showing chart datum (very low water)
⊕	wreck considered dangerous
(7₃) Wk	wreck over which depth, as shown, has been sounded
+++	wreck not considered dangerous
⚓	rock awash at chart datum (very low water)
+	rock barely covered or otherwise dangerous
≈≈≈	overfalls or tide rip
⌇⌇⌇	underwater cable
S	sand
M	mud
Sn	shingle
Sh	shells

Light symbol abbreviations

R	red
G	green
W	white
F	fixed (steady light)
Fl	single flashing
L Fl	long flashing (at least 2 seconds)
Fl(3)	group flashing (groups of 3)
Q	continuous quick flashing
Q(3)	groups of 3 quick flashes
IQ	interrupted quick flashing
VQ	continuous very quick flashing
VQ(3)	groups of 3 very quick flashes
IVQ	interrupted very quick flashing
Oc	occulting (only short periods of darkness)
Iso	isophase (equal periods of dark and lightness)

Squall

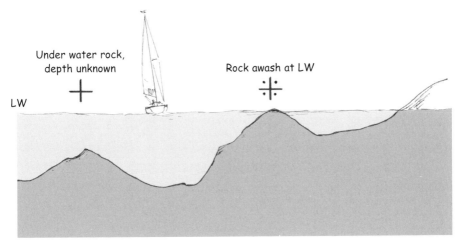

Under water rock, depth unknown

Rock awash at LW

LW

Chart symbols.

Lighthouses

On a metric chart, a small lighthouse might be annotated Fl(2)WRG 10s 14m 7–5M. This means that its light flashes twice every ten seconds; it has three fixed sectors showing white, red and green; it stands 14 metres above high water on a spring tide; and the **luminous range** of its multi-coloured light is from 5 to 7 nautical miles. (Note the possible confusion between lower case m for metres and upper case M for miles.) The luminous range is the distance from which the lighthouse can be seen in clear visibility – which is also the **nominal range** when 'clear' visibility is defined as 10 miles. It's important to realise that the **geographical range** may be different again – that is, the distance at which a powerful light shows above the horizon if your eye level is 15 feet above the water (as it might have been on an old sailing ship). The 'loom' of a powerful lighthouse from seaward is often visible before the actual light rises above the horizon – a fascinating phenomenon that can help fix your position, as we shall see later.

The IALA buoyage system

Navigational buoys are distinguished by shape, colour and the light they show. Their arrangement follows two main principles – lateral and cardinal.

The lateral and cardinal systems

In a **lateral** system (traditionally used in British waters) buoys are laid to port and starboard of the navigable water according to what is known as the conventional direction of buoyage – which runs from SW to NE round the British Isles and then into the various estuaries and rivers. This method lends itself to marking a clearly defined channel, especially in an estuary, like the Thames, where the conventional direction is also the direction of the flood tide and the way into port.

In a **cardinal** system (formerly associated with Continental waters) buoys are distinguished according to the cardinal points of the compass – N, E, S and W – and placed in that direction from the point of interest or danger they mark. This method is particularly suitable for marking, say, the edges of an offshore sandbank or a coastal reef, although it can also mark the features of a channel.

'There's the East Knock.'

The **IALA System A** used in Europe (IALA is the International Association of Lighthouse Authorities) combines both lateral and cardinal principles – port and starboard marks for channels, and mainly cardinal ones for other features.

Lateral marks on the port side of a channel are flat-topped can or pillar buoys, while those to starboard are conical or pointed. They are coloured red to port and green to starboard, as are the lights they show – which match the colours of a ship's navigational sidelights. At night, therefore, it is the colour of a buoy's light that conveys its basic message, rather than the light's rhythm, which varies merely to distinguish individual buoys.

Observed position

Cardinal marks adopt the opposite approach, using the rhythm of the light – which is always white – as well as the buoy's shape and colour to convey its message. These are tall black and yellow buoys with a distinguishing topmark formed by two black cones. We think of the North Pole as the 'top' of the world, so the two cones of a north cardinal topmark both point upwards and those on a south cardinal buoy point downwards (like the traditional gale warning cones). To help remember the west and east topmarks, with their two cones pointing in opposite directions, the shapes they form are often compared to a **W**ineglass and an **E**gg respectively. The black and yellow bands on the buoy's structure (see diagram in centre colour section) have a similar logic to them, though seaweed and rust can sometimes confuse the pattern.

Light characteristics

As for the **light characteristics**, notice that they are arranged rather like a clock face – continuous single flashing for north, a group of three flashes for east at 'three o'clock', six for south (plus a distinguishing long flash) and nine for west. The shorter flashes can be either 'quick' (about once a second) or 'very quick' (twice a second).

An **occulting** light (not to be confused with the occluded front in meteorology) stays lit most of the time, with only short periods of darkness – in other words, the opposite of a flashing light. The description **isophase** (compare with **isobar**) means that the periods of light and dark are equal. It is important to note that these last two characteristics are both associated with safety in the IALA buoyage system. The opposite message comes from the double white flash of a black and red buoy marking an isolated danger, and carrying two black spheres as a topmark.

Three other points to remember about buoys

- They make excellent tidal stream indicators.
- They must have a fair scope of mooring chain to cope with the tidal range, so their position can never be absolutely precise.
- If they are laid to mark a deep-dredged channel for large ships, it is probably sensible for a small, slow-moving yacht to stay outside – in other words, on the 'wrong' side of them.

'No wonder you couldn't find them darling, they're all here!'

The magnetic compass

There are 32 points on a full compass rose, each measuring 11¼° of the circle. But on a modern yacht steering compass, only four (or maybe eight) points are usually marked – N, NE, E, SE, and so on. The primary marking is in degrees from 0° to 360°, probably at intervals of 5°. This is about the smallest margin of error you can hope for in steering a sailing boat, although on the chart you lay a course to the nearest degree.

The course is held by keeping some sort of fore-and-aft lubber line against the required mark on the compass card, or by setting an adjustable steering grid on top of the compass card to the chosen course and then lining up the compass needle – and hence the boat – with it. A grid design with luminous paint might just be usable at night, but most compasses are lit either by a small conventional bulb or by a beta light.

The traditional compass in its binnacle is read from above, but some are designed for mounting in a vertical bulkhead or on top of a coachroof, and can be read from the side. The important thing is to position the compass as far as possible from the magnetic interference of the ferrous metals that are always present in a boat's engine – often in the keel, and in various fittings round the cockpit. You should also avoid putting the compass near electrical equipment such as radios and echo sounders.

Major light

Deviation

However carefully a compass needle is sited, though, it is almost bound to show some **deviation** from the Earth's magnetic pole, if only by a few degrees east or west. A large deviation can be roughtly checked by comparison with a hand bearing compass held well away from possible interference. This will vary with the boat's heading, so accurate navigation – and the yachtmaster's chartwork – require the use of a **deviation card** showing the error in degrees E or W for every couple of compass points or, better still, a curve on which the error associated with any given course can be interpolated. In practice, even a substantial error may not matter on a short coastal trip, although it certainly will on a long sea crossing.

Preparing an accurate card for your own boat is a complicated procedure that involves turning her slowly through successive headings while checking the steering compass against the known bearing of a distant object – or, alternatively, building up a card as opportunities arise during the season. Fortunately, the Yachtmaster course notes provide a standard deviation table.

Variation

Compass work also involves a more fundamental allowance for the **variation** between the direction of the magnetic pole and true north as shown by the lines of longitude. The compass rose printed on a chart is usually two roses, one inside the other, providing both true bearings or courses, and magnetic ones. In our part of the world, a compass needle points slightly west of true north. In the southern North Sea, for example, the present variation is 3° W and slowly decreasing.

It is possible to navigate entirely with magnetic bearings and courses, using the inner ring of the compass rose. The raw data coming from the yacht's steering and hand bearing compasses is, after all, in this form. But the chart grid is laid out on a true basis, and much of the other information you will need – for example, tidal streams – is presented in the same way. So whichever way you work, the problem of **converting from magnetic bearings to true and back again** is going to arise – and in the navigational classroom it occurs only too often! One of the first things to acquire, therefore, is some foolproof way of remembering and checking this procedure.

Look at a compass rose, and you will see that with 3° westerly variation, a magnetic bearing is always that many degrees more than its true equivalent. True north lines up with 3° magnetic (0T=3M), true south lines up with 183° magnetic (180T=183M), and so on. The same would apply if the compass difference was a combination of westerly variation and westerly deviation – say 3° variation and 2° deviation – a total of 5° W to be subtracted from the compass bearing (which in this case, because of its deviation error, is not the same as the

R

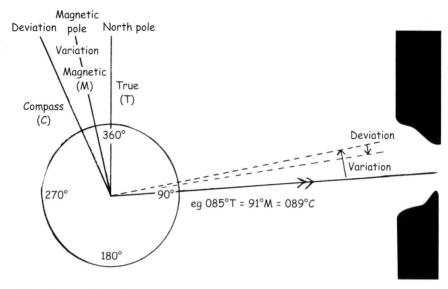

Although some charts for yachtsmen only have magnetic north marked on the compass rose, in the examination you are expected to take account of the variation between magnetic and true north. The magnetic variation for one area can be considered constant – unlike the deviation of the compass needle caused by ferrous metal and electrical fields on board which alters with every heading and can be either east or west. The compass in this diagram should help you to fix this basic principle in your mind. At the top, the destination is true north but both the magnetic variation and compass deviation are pulling the compass needle west.
If your true course is 085° and variation is pulling the compass needle 6° to the West and deviation pulling it back 2° East, your compass course would be 089°.

magnetic bearing) to make it true. True south would now line up with 185° on the compass (180T=185C).

On the other hand, if the compass error is to the east – say an easterly deviation of 5° offset by 3° westerly variation, leaving a net error of 2° E – then the opposite rule will apply. The 2° E must be added to convert a compass reading to true (or, of course, subtracted to convert the other way).

At sea, this particular calculation is usually simpler than it probably looks here. For any given area, variation can be treated as constant, and the more time compass deviation has to work its mischief, the more time you have to get it right. In the classroom, people use various tricks and mnemonics to help them, such as:

Port hand buoy

Variation West, Compass Best,
ADDECT (ADD Easterly Compass to True).

Your instructor will no doubt suggest others. But unless you prefer to work it out from first principles each time, find something that suits you and stick to it.

The log

A log can measure both speed through the water and the distance covered, because of course one determines the other. But it is the latter information that the navigator ultimately needs in order to calculate his position and to check when he should start looking for a landfall.

As the name suggests, this piece of navigational equipment started as a wooden log thrown over the stern on a line, to see how fast the knots marking the line ran out (hence also the nautical term **knots**, meaning nautical miles per hour). Nowadays, the log exists in many forms – **towed (mechanical or electrical), retractable hull-mounted, doppler or ultrasonic**. As with most things, each type has its pros and cons.

The traditional patent log consisted of a counter mounted on the stern rail, driven by a spinner at the end of a line. Obviously this was a simple device with the advantage of no battery to go flat, but was more suited to an ocean passage than coastal cruising (and the rotating line is literally deadly for exhausted migrating birds). Its electronic equivalent – in this case, the spinner generates an electrical current that can be measured – is highly accurate, but it still has to be streamed and recovered.

The modern alternative is to generate the electrical current by a small retractable propeller or paddle wheel mounted through the hull. Once inserted, it is always ready for use, but is easily fouled by weed and mud.

Other logs use the doppler principle – highly accurate, with no holes in the hull or moving parts, but they need careful positioning – or an ultrasonic sensor.

Depth sounding

The traditional method of sounding shallow depths at sea is the **lead line** – a line marked in fathoms with strips of leather and bunting, attached to a lump of lead hollowed out at the bottom and 'armed' with sticky tallow. For routine depth measurement, it has long since been replaced by the echo sounder. Yet the lead still has a useful place on board a yacht: as a back-up; to 'feel' the uneven bottom round an anchorage; to calibrate your echo sounder; or even

fS.M.Sh

to test those chart symbols describing the seabed as mud (M), shells (Sh) or shingle (Sn).

An **echo sounder** works by measuring the time it takes for an ultrasonic pulse emitted by a hull-mounted transducer to be reflected back from the seabed. There are four main types of display – **digital, rotating LED (light emitting diode), dial**, and **trace** – each with its own advantages. Simplest is the digital display in metres or feet. The dial's moving pointer gives a clear sense of changes in depth, while the 'fishfinder' trace shows the seabed contours. The classic in this field is the rotating LED, which clearly shows movement and is easily seen at night, though it does require periodic adjustment to eliminate a secondary echo.

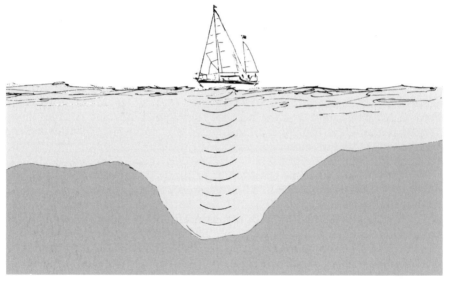

An echo sounder works by measuring how long it takes for an ultrasonic pulse to be reflected back from the seabed. The changing seabed contours help navigation as well as warning of danger.

GPS

The **Global Positioning System (GPS)** provides a constant read-out of a yacht's position – expressed in latitude and longitude – to an accuracy of a few metres.

This navigational miracle is worked by analysing coded signals from a 'birdcage' of US military satellites orbiting the earth. Given a series of such positions, even the most modest GPS computer can instantly work out the yacht's course and speed over the ground, calculate the distance and bearing of any specified waypoint **(WP)** on the chart (such as a navigational buoy), and subsequently the amount by which the yacht deviates from the direct track towards it.

Fine sand with mud and shells

One must admit, going from waypoint to waypoint on autohelm takes the excitement out of sailing.'

Yet the installation that provides all this is less complex (eg in the siting of the aerial) than for a VHF radio. Handheld GPS sets resemble mobile phones.

Any navigator presented with such a remarkable resource might be tempted to believe that it makes traditional methods redundant, and GPS has certainly been eagerly adopted by sailors. However, in truth it is just another electronic aid – albeit an extremely powerful one – that can be deliberately degraded by the Pentagon (as it was in earlier years), or rendered useless by a flat battery. And that is how RYA instructors will regard GPS for the foreseeable future – indeed, you may find there is an exam question illustrating the dangers of relying too heavily on GPS.

Hyperbolic systems

Among the various radio aids to navigation, nowadays radar is rarely carried by sailing yachts, and other systems once favoured by yachtsmen – such as radio beacons and Decca – have largely been phased out. However, the **Loran-C** hyperbolic system is still with us, and Yachtmaster students need to know something about it.

Loran-C works by measuring the time difference between the arrival of radio pulses from a master transmitter and its 'slaves'. Hyperbolic curves of constant difference are plotted as a grid so that two intersecting lines – each representing the relationship between a pair of transmitters – give your position.

The system's accuracy (generally less than that of GPS) varies with range from the transmitters, electrical interference from equipment or thunderstorms, the yacht's position within the grid, and the nature of the surrounding coastline (because the propagation of radio waves is distorted by crossing land).

Tides

Tides are caused by the gravitational pull of the moon and, to a lesser extent, the sun. The orbiting moon produces two high tides every day or, to be a little more precise, in a period of about 24 hours 50 minutes – which is why the time of high water is about 50 minutes later each day.

When the moon is full, or new, the sun's gravitational pull is exerted in the same direction. The movement of water is greater, tidal streams run faster, and the tide rises higher (and falls lower) than at other times. Such conditions are known as **spring tides**. They occur every two weeks, in keeping with the phases of the moon; and at any given place on the coast, high water springs will be at roughly the same time of day.

But in alternate weeks, when the sun is pulling at right angles to the moon, the tidal range from high to low water is smaller. These are **neap tides** – less useful if you are trying to float your boat out of a mud berth, but also less of a hazard when crossing a shallow bar at low water. Spring tides, incidentally, are especially high and low during the spring and in the autumn.

Depths shown on a chart are measured from a level known as the **chart datum** – either the mean level of low water spring tides (MLWS) or, more commonly, the level of the lowest astronomically predictable tide (LAT). The height of a tide is also measured from the chart datum, as is the height of a drying sandbank. But note that the height of a lighthouse is measured from mean high water springs (MHWS) – a point easily forgotten when facing an exam question about the distance at which the light is visible.

At the centre of this oscillating pattern of rising and falling tides is a **mean level** (ML).

Tide tables

The primary source of tidal predictions is the *Admiralty Tide Tables*. Volume 1 of this covers British waters, although tide tables are also available in many local publications and in **nautical almanacs** produced for yachtsmen.

The widely used *Macmillan Reeds* almanac, for instance, provides compre-

Water track

Definitions of the various tidal levels.

hensive tidal data for British and Continental waters, plus information on a vast range of other subjects – navigation (including passage planning, way-points, tidal streams, pilotage and harbour charts), radio aids, weather fore-casting, collision regulations, safety procedures and first aid. The almanac makes a plausible claim to contain all the nautical information needed to navi-gate British and European waters from Denmark to Gibraltar. At sea, therefore, such a publication is invaluable. In the classroom, too, it is a reasonable answer to give for almost any question about sources of information.

Opening the Admiralty **tide tables** at the pages dealing with the 'standard port' of Dover, you will find the times and heights of high and low water for each day of the year (times in Universal Time, heights in metres). Associated with the table is a steeply humped **tidal curve** – or, to be more precise, two curves superimposed: a solid line for springs and a dashed line for neaps.

Tidal curves

These curves are the basis of the Admiralty method of tide calculation you will use for Yachtmaster exams. Note that their height is not marked directly in metres, but in proportional factors ranging from zero to 1.0 – at high tide,

'I thought you did all this at night school – working out tides, times, ranges . . .'

because the 'shape' of the tide is determined separately from its height. A horizontal scale across the base of the curves shows the time before and after high water. Until the curves are applied to the actual heights for a particular day, plotted on the left-hand side of the diagram, they merely show, for example, that on a rising spring tide at Dover, the water will rise by less than a tenth of its eventual range (a factor of less than 0.1) during the first hour (four hours before HW, not five, because this asymmetrical tide takes less time to rise than it does to fall). After five hours of a falling neap tide, the level will be down to about two-tenths of the range (a factor of 0.2), and so on.

Similar curves are shown for each of the **standard ports**. Some curves are quite symmetrical; others are sharply skewed. For ports in the Bristol Channel, where the tidal range is enormous, they are steeply peaked. On the east coast they are much flatter. For spring tides at Southampton the peak is double, indicating a second high water, because of the complex way that tides flow round the Isle of Wight and the surrounding area.

Rule of Twelfths

If you were to take all these individual curves and combine them in a single smooth symmetrical line – that is, the ideal pattern the tide would follow if there were nothing to distort its flow – that line could be expressed as a simple

Isophase light (Iso) – equal light and dark periods

rule: the tide would rise or fall approximately one-twelfth of its range in the first hour after low or high water, two-twelfths in the second hour, three-twelfths in the third and fourth hours, two-twelfths again in the fifth hour, and one-twelfth in the sixth and final hour.

So if you find tidal calculations confusing (and, let's face it, many fine yachtsmen have no head for figures), you can fall back on this **Rule of Twelfths**: 1, 2, 3, 3, 2, 1.

On many occasions such a simple pattern will obviously be less accurate than

first hour

second

third

fourth

fifth

sixth

The Rule of Twelfths. In this case the yacht is crossing the shoal two and a half hours after high water. In another hour, the shoal would be awash.

the full calculation, especially where the tidal range is large or the shape asymmetrical. But then there are other sources of error in tidal predictions. A rise of only about 11 millibars in atmospheric pressure will lower the sea level by a tenth of a metre. A storm surge driving down the North Sea can raise tides by a metre or more above their predicted level. Local effects are also powerful. At the head of an estuary, the incoming tide may arrive with great suddenness (the Severn bore is an extreme example) while the first of the ebb may rush away with surprising speed. Therefore a generous safety margin is always required, not least because near real rocks, or on a real bar, your boat will be bouncing up and down in the waves!

Back in the classroom, though, you will have to face an assessment paper that treats the tidal predictions as exact to a tenth of a metre, so you have to get the **Admiralty method** clear in your mind.

Making tidal calculations

To find the height of tide (at a standard port) **at a given time** between high and low water:

1 Calculate how many hours before or after HW your given time is, and mark it along the base of the curves (A).
2 From this starting point, draw a line vertically to meet the appropriate curve (springs or neaps) (A1).
3 Proceed horizontally to meet the sloping tide line showing the relevant range on the required day (A2).
4 Proceed vertically, up or down, to read off the height at your given time (A3).

To find the time at which the tide will reach a given height (at a standard port):

1 Starting from the required height on the horizontal height scale (B), draw a line vertically to meet the sloping tide line (B1).
2 Proceed horizontally to the appropriate curve (springs or neaps, rising or falling) (B2).
3 Proceed vertically down to read off the time before or after HW on the horizontal time scale (B3).

'According to my calculations, there's plenty of water.'

East cardinal buoy

DOVER

MEAN SPRING AND NEAP CURVES

Springs occur 2 days after New and Full Moon.

Extract from the Admiralty Tide Tables Vol 1 NP 201-02.

RW

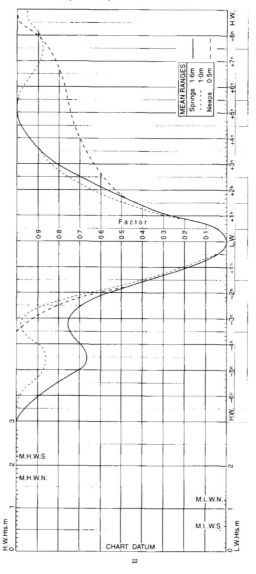

POOLE HARBOUR
MEAN SPRING AND NEAP CURVES
Springs occur 2 days after New and Full Moon.

Extract from the Admiralty Tide Tables Vol 1 NP 201-02.

Safe water mark

There will obviously be many occasions when a calculation of the range(HW–LW) shows neither a spring nor a neap tide, but something in between. If the two curves for that port are significantly different, interpolate between them by eye, after checking the actual range against the ranges shown for springs and neaps.

Tidal curves for **secondary ports** are not normally available, so consult an almanac for time and height corrections to be applied to the appropriate standard-port curve. Bear in mind that the corrections vary according to the time and height of high or low water (whether it is springs or neaps), so there may be more interpolating to be done, graphically or otherwise.

For those sailing on the south coast of England, there is one other complication. Between Swanage and Selsey Bill, the shape of the tides is grossly distorted – so much so that, as we have seen, there may be a double high tide. Fortunately, low tide remains a single, clearly identified event, so tidal curves in this area are centred on LW. For some of these ports a third 'critical' curve is included because the shape of the spring and neap curves is so different.

Points to remember about tidal calculations

The practical seagoing message where tidal calculations are concerned is to match your method to the circumstances. Before crossing an exposed bar on a fast flowing ebb, it is obviously worth taking more trouble with your arithmetic, and allowing a bigger safety margin, than when easing into a muddy estuary on the flood.

Tidal streams

Information on tidal streams comes in two main forms: special little chartlets that may be made up into a **tidal stream atlas**, and **tidal diamonds**, which refer to a table of direction and speed.

On a set of chartlets (as found in an *Admiralty Tidal Stream Atlas*, in almanacs and on some charts) the streams at each hour before and after HW at a certain port are shown by a pattern of arrows marked with the rate in knots at springs and neaps. The arrows vary in thickness according to the strength of the tide. This presentation gives an excellent general impression.

Tidal diamonds are marked on the chart, and identified by letters. These refer to tables showing the **rate and direction** at each hour. (In case you come across the more traditional terms, the direction of a tide is sometimes referred to as the **set**, while the rate is the **drift**.) This presentation is convenient for plotting a course, because the direction of the tide can be read straight off as a true bearing (that is, the direction in which the tidal stream is flowing, not the direction from which it has come, as with wind).

Extract from the Admiralty Tidal Stream Atlas for the Solent: one hour before
high water Portsmouth.

Wreck visible at low water

Points to remember about tidal streams

- They run stronger in deep water.
- They tend to set into bays, and in the lee of a headland may even eddy in the reverse direction.
- They can be accelerated into tide rips or races where they have to force their way past headlands like Portland and the Lizard, or squeeze through a bottleneck like the notorious Pentland Firth. On a spring ebb, even the sandy river bars of the east coast can produce standing waves that will fill a yacht's cockpit. A big race produces alarming, unpredictable waves even in calm weather and, if it is blowing, they should definitely be avoided – unless, as sometimes happens, there is a calm eddying patch close inshore through which you can slip.

Other basic sources of information

Before moving on to the application of tidal streams, and to chartwork in general, there are one or two other basic sources of which you should be aware.

The *Admiralty List of Lights and Fog Signals* is the big-ship equivalent of the information on navigational aids that you will find in yachting almanacs. A point to remember here is that the bearings of lights – for example, to indicate the sector over which a lighthouse shows red or white – are recorded as they appear from seaward.

The Admiralty also publishes a long series of **sailing directions or pilots**, authoritative works of reference traditionally famous for their little sketches of the coastline (now replaced by colour photographs) and grim warnings to navigators. But again these are written mainly for ships, not yachts. You may find the *Cruising Association Handbook* more useful; this gives detailed pilotage information for approaching and berthing in a wide range of European ports and harbours. Or you may prefer one of the many very detailed pilot books that cover particular areas.

Chartwork

Instruments

Essential instruments needed for chartwork:
- Ruler (the longest you can find, preferably made of transparent plastic
- Parallel rule (the roller kind are fine in the classroom, but not on a yacht) for transferring bearings from a compass rose to another part of the chart
- Some sort of course plotter (such as the Breton, the Portland or the Douglas protractor)
- A pair of one-handed dividers for measuring distance (from the latitude scale)
- A pair of compasses for drawing arcs
- A couple of soft hexagonal pencils and a big soft rubber (hard pencils and a small harsh rubber will soon destroy the surface on frequently used corners of the practice chart)

The **symbols** you should use as you come to them are:

△   **estimated position (EP)**

⊙   **observed position** or **fix** (position obtained from position lines)

—→—   **water track** (wake course, allowing for leeway)

—»—   **ground track** (course made good relative to land)

—»»—   **tidal stream** or **current**

——→   **position line**

«——»   **transferred position line**

Nearly all the problems you will be asked to solve on the practice chart are variants of three basic geometrical calculations – fixing the yacht's position, working out the course to reach a given position, and deciding where you have actually arrived after steering a given course for a certain distance. The last of these could theoretically be the **dead reckoning**, which makes no allowance for tidal offset and leeway, but is much more likely to be an **estimated position**, which does makes these allowances.

Eddies

Obtaining a fix

To obtain a fix you need at least two position lines, preferably at a broad angle. These are the lines along which the yacht's position must lie, so that if they intersect, and they are accurate, then there is only one place the boat can be.

The **GPS** does this instantly by displaying the lines of latitude and longitude that define your position. But there are many other sources that will confirm or substitute for this device. The most commonly used is the hand **compass bearing** of a visible object marked on the chart – a buoy, a light, or a tower that matches the chartmaker's traditional description 'conspic.'. This may be combined with another compass bearing or with some other source: the extended **transit** between two visible objects; the **distance off** a coastline (as shown, for example, on a radar screen); the **dipping distance** of a lighthouse at night; a **line of soundings** – or even a single sounding if it establishes a position on a clearly defined seabed contour. In an emergency, the Coastguard may be able to give the bearing of your VHF radio transmission.

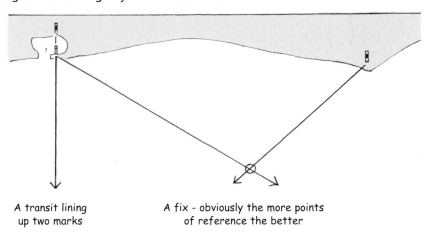

A transit lining
up two marks

A fix - obviously the more points
of reference the better

Position lines for a fix can be obtained from a compass bearing,
a transit, distance off, or a line of soundings.

Using a couple of position lines is the principle you instinctively apply when sailing past, say, a pier, and you think: 'We're about two miles off, steering roughly parallel with the shore, and the pier's abeam, so we must be about . . . there on the chart'.

A common dodge for improving on guesswork for the distance off is known as **doubling the angle on the bow**. If you take a bearing of an object on the shore ahead and then maintain a steady course until the angle between bearing and course has doubled (see diagram), the three lines plotted on the chart form a triangle with two equal sides. Equipped with a log and a tidal atlas, you know the length of one of those sides – the distance the yacht has covered – and that is also the distance off.

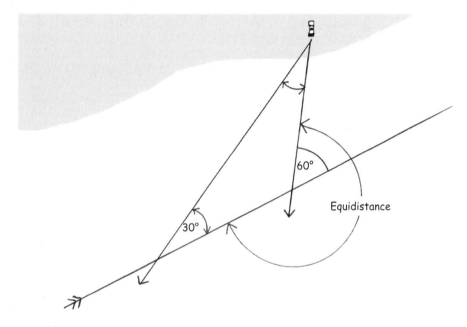

Doubling the angle on the bow. If a bearing is taken on a known point to find the angle it makes from the ship's bow (in this case 30°) and another taken when that figure is doubled (ie 60°), the distance between the two points from which the bearings were taken will be the same as the ship's distance from the known point.

One combination of position lines that ships used before the days of radar, and which can still be useful aboard a yacht, is the **bearing of a lighthouse at night and its dipping distance**. As we all know, the curvature of the earth makes distant objects fall below the horizon. And the distance at which this happens to a lighthouse of a given height, plus the observer's own height above sea level, can be found from tables provided in nautical almanacs. The position line obtained in this way is a circle round the light whose radius is that total distance. A compass bearing of the light, intersecting the circle, gives a fix.

Position of tabulated tidal stream

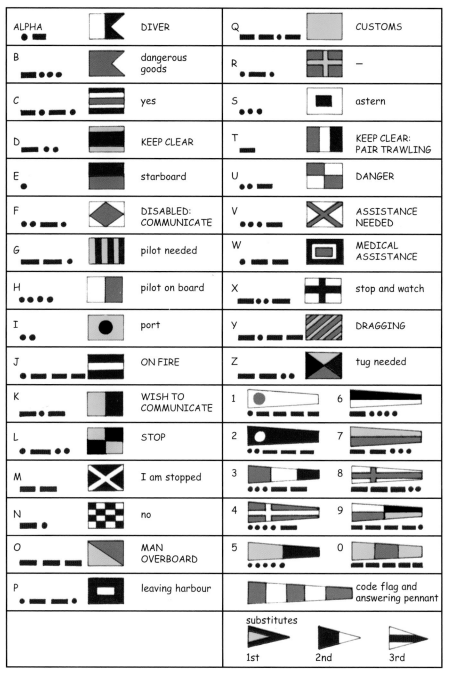

ALPHA ● ▬		DIVER	Q ▬ ▬ ● ▬		CUSTOMS
B ▬ ● ● ●		dangerous goods	R ● ▬ ●		–
C ▬ ● ▬ ●		yes	S ● ● ●		astern
D ▬ ● ●		KEEP CLEAR	T ▬		KEEP CLEAR: PAIR TRAWLING
E ●		starboard	U ● ● ▬		DANGER
F ● ● ▬ ●		DISABLED: COMMUNICATE	V ● ● ● ▬		ASSISTANCE NEEDED
G ▬ ▬ ●		pilot needed	W ● ▬ ▬		MEDICAL ASSISTANCE
H ● ● ● ●		pilot on board	X ▬ ● ● ▬		stop and watch
I ● ●		port	Y ▬ ● ▬ ▬		DRAGGING
J ● ▬ ▬ ▬		ON FIRE	Z ▬ ▬ ● ●		tug needed
K ▬ ● ▬		WISH TO COMMUNICATE	1		6
L ● ▬ ● ●		STOP	2		7
M ▬ ▬		I am stopped	3		8
N ▬ ●		no	4		9
O ▬ ▬ ▬		MAN OVERBOARD	5		0
P ● ▬ ▬ ●		leaving harbour			code flag and answering pennant
			substitutes 1st 2nd 3rd		

Morse Code, the International Code of Signals, and reminders of their joint meanings.
Those in capitals may be worth memorising.

CARDINAL MARKS

VQ or Q

VQ(9)10s
or Q(9)15s

VQ(3)5s
or Q(3)10s

VQ(6) + LFl10s or
Q(6) + LFl15s

The characteristics of cardinal buoys are easily remembered. The top marks point up (North), down (South), together (West, like a wineglass), and the one with bases together must be East (like an egg). The black sections of the buoy are also where the top marks point. The characteristics of the lights are as on a clock face: three, six and nine. The odd one out – instead of twelve, one.

Special mark – shape optional – has a yellow light (any rhythm)

Isolated danger mark could be a buoy of any shape; light white Gp Fl (2) – remember 2 spheres and Gp Fl (2)

LATERAL MARKS

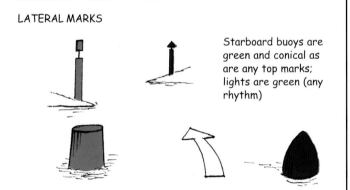

Starboard buoys are green and conical as are any top marks; lights are green (any rhythm)

Safe water mark can also be a spherical buoy or beacon; light is white isophase, occulting or one long flash every 10 seconds

Lateral buoys are usually related to the flood tide with; port hand buoys are red and flat topped, as are any top marks; lights are red (any rhythm).

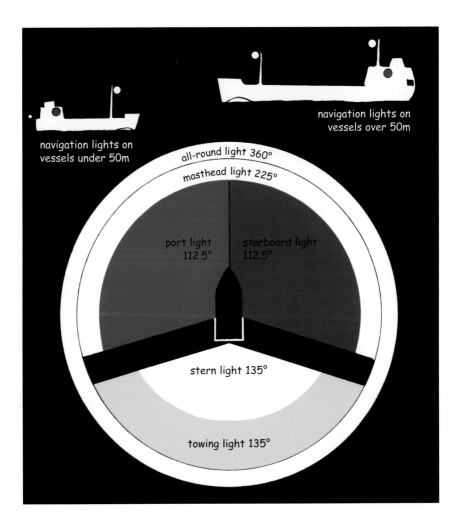

navigation lights on
vessels over 50m

navigation lights on
vessels under 50m

all-round light 360°

masthead light 225°

port light
112.5°

starboard light
112.5°

stern light 135°

towing light 135°

An easy way to remember the arcs of the navigation lights is that the stern light covers an arc made up of the first three odd numbers - 1, 3, 5 - 135°. Subtract this from 360° and you have the arc of the masthead light - 225°. Halve this and you have the arcs of the port and starboard lights - 112.5°. The all-round light is 360°.

POWER DRIVEN VESSELS UNDER WAY

bow view of vessel less than 50m   port   stern

bow view of vessel more than 50m   the number of masthead lights - two compulsory over 50m but only one compulsory under 50m - indicate the vessel's length whatever her type   stern

air cushion vessel – bow view   port less than 50m   stern   vessel under 7m - white all-round light

TOWING AND PUSHING

bow   tug less than 50m with length of tow more than 200m

  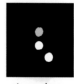

bow tug more than 50m   day signal   stern view, any length

tug more than 50m with length of tow more than 200m

bow

port of vessel less than 50m pushing ahead

stern

bow of vessel less than 50m towing alongside

port side of vessel more than 50m

stern

bow

port

stern

sailing vessel making way

FISHING VESSELS

bow of trawler not making way

port side of trawler more than 50m making way

day signal

not making way

surface net fishing vessel making way - port side

stern making way

bow not making way

making way - port side, nets extending more than 150m from vessel

stern making way (additional light shows direction of gear)

day signal

bow view - not under command

day signal (balls up?)

port side - not under command but making way

bow - vessel restricted in ability to manoeuvre

port side and making way

stern and making way

day signal (think of the diamond as the vessel that is restricted)

bow - anchored vessel restricted in her ability to manoeuvre

port side - more than 50m

day signal

bow - vessel less than 50m, towing and unable to deviate from her course

port (same red, white, red as above)

stern

MINE SWEEPERS

day signals

day signal

bow making way

DREDGERS

bow not making way (double red lights indicate obstructed side)

day signal

When the size of the vessel prevents these shapes being shown, a vessel engaged in under-water operations should fly the code flag A

VESSELS CONSTRAINED BY THEIR DRAUGHT

bow

more than 50m – port side

stern

day signal

PILOT VESSELS

bow - at anchor

at anchor - less than 50m - port side

stern - making way

more than 50m

day signal - the red and white of the all-round lights are duplicated in the day signal

ANCHORED VESSELS AND VESSELS AGROUND

at anchor - more than 50m - port side

day signal

bow

aground - less than 50m

stern

day signal

aground – more than 50m (note preponderance of port red lights)

SEAPLANES

bow

port side

stern

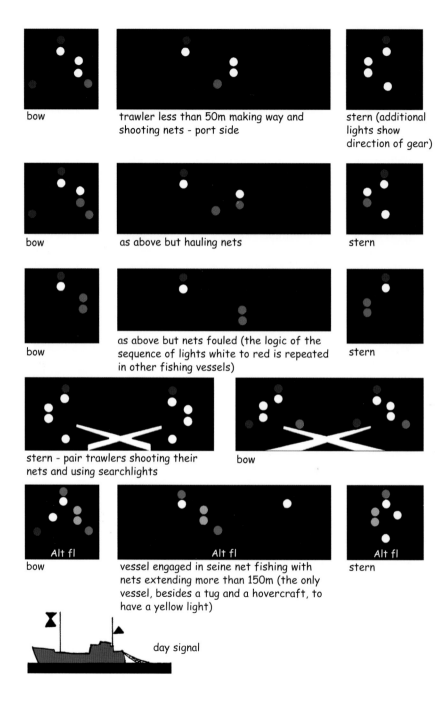

bow

trawler less than 50m making way and shooting nets - port side

stern (additional lights show direction of gear)

bow

as above but hauling nets

stern

bow

as above but nets fouled (the logic of the sequence of lights white to red is repeated in other fishing vessels)

stern

stern - pair trawlers shooting their nets and using searchlights

bow

Alt fl

bow

Alt fl

vessel engaged in seine net fishing with nets extending more than 150m (the only vessel, besides a tug and a hovercraft, to have a yellow light)

Alt fl

stern

day signal

Two points to remember about this calculation

- The charted height of a lighthouse is measured from MHWS, so if it is not high water you have to add on the difference between that and the actual tidal level before consulting the distance table.
- Do not be caught out by the examiner suggesting the use of dipping distance when the yacht is still beyond the light's luminous range.

A general warning about compass bearings – avoid taking them from objects like headlands and hills; these may look clearcut from seaward, but their precise location on a two-dimensional chart is difficult to establish. Also, to reiterate a point made earlier, avoid shallow angles between bearings because they increase the margin of error. Remember too that a **back bearing** from something you have passed may be just as useful as one taken from an object you are approaching – although, in practice, people often forget to look behind them.

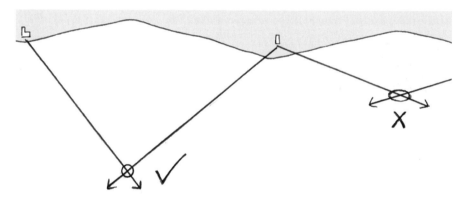

Right and wrong fix. A right angle between bearings reduces the margin of error. Very broad – or narrow – angles increase it.

Leading marks.

Transits

A transit (preferably between objects a good distance apart) can be extremely useful just on its own. The classic application is a pair of **leading marks** or leading lights to show the safest way into a harbour or the best water over a difficult bar. To take other examples of which RYA examiners are fond: two objects might be chosen so that as long as one is kept 'open' of the other (that is, not in transit), the yacht will stay clear of sandbanks lining the entrance to a bay; or the appearance of a transit might be used as a kind of visual alarm clock, to remind

'Ease her down Joe, I've just lost the leading marks.'

Cold front

the helmsman when to change course. Remember it takes only a moment to record a transit with the time it appeared – it may suddenly be needed.

Clearing lines and running fixes

Individual compass bearings can be used to provide **clearing lines** beyond which you must not go if you are to clear rocks or shoals, or to mark a safe turning point. Whatever their purpose, visual bearings will almost always be inaccurate – as you will clearly be reminded when three of them produce not a precise intersection, but a triangular 'cocked hat'. Your boat is probably in the middle of it, but if the position is critical, assume the worst case – or take some fresh bearings.

Even if only one identifiable object is visible, it may be possible to establish what is known as a **running fix**, by taking two successive bearings. The first is plotted and the log mileage at that time recorded. After a suitable interval a second bearing of the same object is taken, and the course made good during the interval – allowing for the tidal stream – is plotted from any point on the first bearing or position line. This first line is then transferred (see diagram) so as to mark the only point on the second line where the track made good actually fits between the two bearings. That must be the yacht's position.

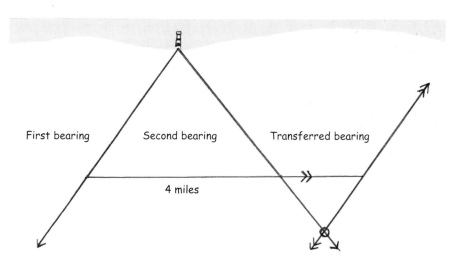

First bearing   Second bearing   Transferred bearing

4 miles

A running fix. Take a bearing from a known point and plot it on the chart. Then run a recorded distance (4 miles in this example) and take a second bearing. Transfer the first bearing 4 miles to intersect the second. Your fix is where the two position lines cross.

Plotting a course

If you steer due north by your boat's compass then it is extremely unlikely that you will actually travel in a true northerly direction over the ground. To start with, the compass is pointing not to true north, but to the magnetic pole (the variation we discussed earlier), and it almost certainly has some additional deviation. If yours is a sailing boat with the wind ahead or on the beam, she will also be making leeway – that is, moving slightly crabwise, perhaps 5° downwind of the direction her bows are pointing. And she will also be affected by the tidal stream.

Much of the chartwork in this part of the course would be much simpler if there were no such things as tidal streams. These may carry your boat bodily sideways – as if on a moving carpet – and turn the straight line of your course into a potentially confusing triangle of velocities. In practice, the actual course may be a shallow curve. Charts and tidal atlases enable the navigator to shape a course and plot it to allow for tide.

The tide may simply help her along or cancel out some of her progress through the water (a boat moving at 4½ knots with a 1½ knot tide under her travels twice as fast over the ground as the same boat heading into the tide – 6 knots instead of 3 – which is why it is so important for small craft to work their tides). However, the stream sometimes sets across your course, altering hour by hour, and this has to be allowed for (along with the other factors mentioned above) when **plotting the ground track**, or course made good over the ground. The following method is illustrated in the diagram on the top of page 33:

1 Add or subtract deviation to convert compass course (C) to magnetic (M).
2 Subtract westerly variation to convert magnetic course (M) to true (T).

Yacht harbour, marina

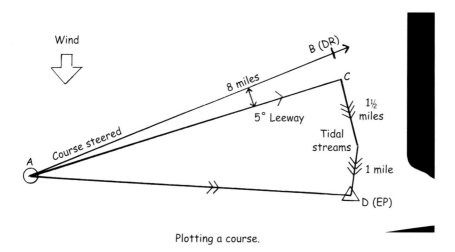

Plotting a course.

3 Lay off the resulting true course steered from the observed position A; measure the distance run through the water against the adjacent latitude scale (in this example 8 miles in 2 hours) and mark it off to give position B – the 'dead reckoning'.
4 Apply leeway downwind (in this example 5°) and label the resulting water track to position C.
5 Look up the direction and rate of the tidal stream during these same two hours and lay them off from C as two successive '**vectors**', one for each hour, so as to establish the estimated position D.
6 Connect A and D to give an approximation of the yacht's track and complete the 'velocity triangle'.

The accuracy of the estimated position will depend on, among other things, the accuracy of the helmsman's steering, the allowance for leeway (which varies with the type of boat and the set of the sails), the log reading, and the tidal stream predictions – so, as you can see, small boat navigation is definitely not an exact science.

Shaping a course from one given position to another

In a sense this is the same triangular problem in reverse: anticipating the effect of tide and leeway instead of working it out after the event. Again the method is shown in the diagram on page 34 (notice – because this is often a source of misunderstanding – that the yacht's progress along her track AB is *not* measured off from the starting point A, but from the end of the tidal vector C):

'Relax I've got a backbearing that clears everything.'

1 Lay off the desired ground track from A to B.
2 Calculate roughly how long the trip will take (in this example, something over two hours) and lay off the appropriate tidal vectors to point C.
3 With compasses set to the distance the yacht will cover during the same two hours, strike an arc from C through the desired ground track AB and mark it D, so that CD is the water track required to reach the nearest practical point to B.
4 Compare the water track with the magnetic compass rose and label it.
5 Apply the appropriate corrections for leeway and deviation (both of which you will be given in an exam) to obtain the compass course to steer.

Shaping a course.

Fix

And after you've got the matches, just ask casually what lighthouse it is.'

This rather clumsy procedure actually takes the yacht in a shallow meandering curve from A to D. If it is necessary to stay close to the track from A to B – for example, to avoid straying into shallow water – each hour's tidal stream could be plotted to produce a separate course to steer. Alternatively, as here, a succession of tidal vectors can be plotted end to end to produce a single mean course to steer for the whole trip. As you near B, so you must plot your EP and adjust course to hit it off exactly – or to be safe, aim a bit uptide.

GPS, through its **cross track function**, is making similar sorts of calculation all the time, without knowing why. Having entered B as a waypoint, the size and direction of the cross track error (XTE) tells you what course correction to apply. If the waypoint bearing given by the GPS remains constant, you are on a 'collision course'. But, as with any electronic aid to navigation, it obviously pays to have an independent means of estimating your position from time to time, until eventually you get a visual bearing or transit from your destination.

There are some simple cases – for example, a passage across the North Sea or the Channel that is expected to last about 12 hours, with a fair wind – when it is actually more efficient to ignore the tide. Rather than fight to stay on the direct ground track, it will pay you to steer a direct course through the water, allowing the yacht to be swept first to one side of the track and then the other by the tide, in an S-shaped curve whose shape is related to the tidal curves mentioned earlier. This assumes that the effects of the tidal ebb and flow roughly cancel out.

In other situations the tide should be allowed for positively. For example, when tacking across a tidal stream, it pays to set off up-tide, so you are lifted up to windward by it – a tactic known as 'lee-bowing'. The boat's sideways movement will free the apparent wind.

Allowing for a tidal stream is also crucial when tacking across the tide to clear a headland or round a buoy, as you often do when racing. If necessary, plot the ground track required by applying a tidal correction to the water track dictated by the wind, then go about when you come on to that bearing.

The ship's log

There are many different reasons for keeping a log, among them the possibility of GPS failure or the sudden onset of fog, and various types of log result. A motor yacht's log, for example, might include a record of rpm, temperature, charging rate and fuel state that would not be needed aboard a sailing vessel. The universal requirement is always to have some way of plotting the yacht's position, or reworking a doubtful calculation, from a basic record of time, course, speed, navigational marks and so on. On a large vessel where the crew is organised into watches, a log helps to tell the new watch what has been happening while they were below. In any case, potential Yachtmasters need a record of their seatime to obtain that important certificate!

Points to remember about navigation

- Never miss an easy chance to fix your position, eg from a transit.
- Cardinal buoys follow the clock face, and lateral ones match your navigation lights.
- Variation West, Compass Best.
- Don't waste a favourable tide – even if it means getting up extra early!
- The Rule of Twelfths – 1, 2, 3, 3, 2, 1.
- Adapt your navigation to the circumstances, eg a falling tide or doubtful visibility.

Rock awash at chart datum

Weather

Apart from the sheer pleasure of understanding our daily weather, the study of meteorology is obviously extremely important for sailors.

On passage, we need to recognise the first signs of an approaching depression, with its rain, gales and wind shifts. When racing inshore, we have to make use of more local effects, like the summer sea breezes. Preparing for Yachtmaster exams, we also need to know something of meteorological theory, with its special language. We may even want to draw our own weather maps.

Fortunately, much of the forecasters' technical jargon is already familiar from the newspaper weather maps, radio and television. Indeed, the BBC shipping forecast is almost a national institution! We are used to looking at patterns of 'isobars' or hearing about 'advancing depressions' and 'associated troughs'. There are even satellite pictures of the swirling clouds that mark their progress. With this background, the meteorology section of the RYA course is simply a matter of going back to first principles and working through them coherently, learning the definitions as you go.

The basic weather system and terms used

In describing the weather, the most fundamental distinction we make is between a warm day and a cold one. And, in truth, temperature ultimately determines the other characteristics that interest us – whether it is wet or dry, sunny or cloudy, windy or calm.

In north-west Europe we live roughly on the boundary of the cold air masses of the polar regions and the warm air of the tropics. The line where they meet is known as the **polar front**.

The density of air varies with its temperature, so a warm pocket of air tends to float to the top of the surrounding cooler mass, just as a cold pocket of air descends. The movement set up by this tendency for warmer air to rise – sometimes a complete circulation – is known as **convection**. As the air rises it cools, which is one way that the invisible vapour carried by any air, but especially warm air – which can carry more of it – condenses into visible droplets of cloud or fog. Convective cumulus cloud, which is the fluffy white kind seen in children's picture books, is a result of this process. Any other cooling process will have a similar effect, although the visual result may be quite different.

In other words, the amount of water vapour that air can absorb before it becomes saturated increases with temperature. As cooling air reaches this varying point of saturation, it is said to be at the **dew point**. If it gets any cooler, the excess water vapour will condense.

The warm moist air inside your car mists over a cold windscreen because the glass cools it below its dew point. More relevantly, warm moist air advancing from subtropical regions across colder northern seas – from the Azores into the Western Approaches, for example – will tend to release its excess moisture as fog. This consists of water droplets, just like the convective cloud, but we give it a different name because the air from which it condenses is cooler than the mass above. There is no convective tendency to rise, so the fog characteristically drifts near the surface.

In general, a mixed air mass, with the cooler, denser air at the bottom, is going to be stable. One with warmer, less dense air temporarily trapped at its base will be unstable – a characteristic of polar air masses moving south over warmer seas. So the polar front, along which moving air masses of different temperatures tend to meet and swirl, is also likely to be an area of complex instability.

A **depression**, the most prominent single feature of the weather along the coastlines of north-west Europe, often starts as no more than a ripple on the polar front way out in the Atlantic. A bulge of warm subtropical air pushes into and over a cooler northern air mass and begins to swirl upwards. The bulge becomes a moving wave, with a **warm front** on its leading edge, and a **cold front** on its trailing edge as cooler air closes in behind it. And if, as often happens, the cold front eventually overtakes the warm front, cutting off its supply of warm air, the fronts are said to be **occluded**.

The depression, centred on the crest of the wave, is therefore an area of ascending air and low pressure, and commonly referred to simply as a '**low**'. A complete area of relatively high pressure, where cool air is gently descending, is known as an **anticyclone** (the opposite word, cyclone, being reserved for vigorous tropical depressions) or just a '**high**'.

Pressure can be measured with a **barometer** (the compact aneroid kind is the type most usually found on yachts) and shown on a scale divided into millibars. The pressures we are concerned with fluctuate around the 1000 millibar level, with less than 940 millibars in a really deep 'low', and more than 1040 millibars in an intense 'high' (that is a 100 millibar range). Two lows are often said to be divided by a **ridge of high pressure**. Within a depression, pressure is especially low along the line of the two fronts, which are therefore important examples of what is known as a **trough**.

Meteorologists illustrate and analyse these features by drawing maps, **synoptic charts**, covered in isobars – that is, lines of equal barometric pressure. The effect is to show the contours of a depression or anticyclone, just as height contours on a land map show the shape of a range of hills.

On a weather map they also show the direction of the wind, because in the

Beaufort 1 – light air

northern hemisphere **air circulates anticlockwise round a depression**, along the contours but slightly inwards towards the centre, while round an anticyclone it circulates in the opposite direction: clockwise and slightly outwards.

The contours of a depression tend to be steeper than those of an anticyclone, especially near its centre, and this shows up on the map in the closer spacing of the isobars. The winds are correspondingly stronger, often up to gale force and beyond, which is of course why yachtsmen should be on their guard against the approach of a deep low. In any case, the rain and drizzle that usually accompany its passing fronts put it in the general category of bad weather, whereas a stationary anticyclone is often the source of a fine spell of summer weather.

Not all depressions come in from the Atlantic. For example, in hot summer weather a thundery low sometimes forms in France and spreads across the Channel to bring its clouds into southern England. But the classic pattern of British weather – and certainly the one most relevant to passing the Yachtmaster meteorology exam – is caused by a depression tracking north-east across the British Isles until it disappears somewhere over the Baltic. The clouds that signal its approach, the falling barometer, the **wind shifts** marking its contours – these are all the basis of those old weather sayings about mackerel skies, the moon hiding her head in a halo, and winds that shift against the sun.

Look at an isobaric chart of a symmetrical low, and you will see that if it passes directly overhead, moving north-east, the wind will shift through 180° after a brief lull – roughly from south-east to north-west (in our diagram on page 40, the observer's viewpoint moves along track A). If the centre of low pressure passes to the north (track B), a southerly wind will **veer – that is, shift in a clockwise direction** – until it becomes westerly. If the low passes to the south (track C), the wind will **back – anticlockwise** – from an easterly to a northerly direction. The barometer will fall and rise during the same period.

If you draw the chart a little more realistically to show the deeper troughs of low pressure accompanying the advancing warm and cold fronts, the wind shifts will be sharper at these points, especially at the passage of the cold front. And if this primary low has a secondary one developing on the tail of the cold front – perhaps more violent than its parent – the wind may back sharply only to veer again:

When the wind shifts against the sun,
Trust it not for back 'twill run.

Patterns of falling and rising pressure can be traced in the same way, for example at the cold front:

When rise commences after low,
Squalls expect and then clear blow.

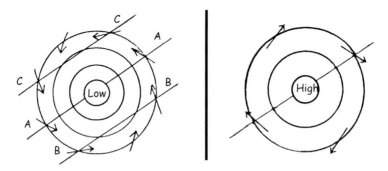

Above: The basic wind patterns of 'low'
and 'high' in the northern hemisphere.
Below: Additional features in
practice – fronts, and a secondary depression.

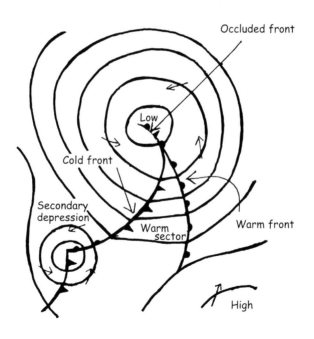

Ground track

But the first signs of an approaching depression are likely to be visual – the wispy 'mares' tails' driven far ahead of it by strong, high altitude winds:

> *Mackerel sky and mares' tails,*
> *Make tall ships carry small sails.*

Clouds

Meteorologists distinguish clouds according to their height and form, using the **Latin words cumulus** (heap), **stratus** (blanket), and **cirrus** (curl of hair) to describe heaped-up, layered and high wispy cloud respectively. The word **alto** may be added to indicate a medium-level cloud of some particular form, and **nimbus** (storm cloud) means rain-bearing. But the resulting classification is not totally logical, so you just have to learn the main types.

Clouds to remember

- **Cumulus (Cu)** – low, mainly white clouds piled into small heaps, usually associated with fine weather.
- **Stratocumulus (Sc)** – low heaped clouds gathered into an extensive layer.
- **Cumulonimbus (Cb)** – towering heaps of cloud that produce showers or thunderstorms.
- **Stratus (St)** – low layer of featureless grey cloud.
- **Nimbostratus (Ns)** – layers of dark rain-bearing cloud.
- **Altocumulus (Ac)** – medium-level heaped clouds in rounded, lens-shaped or castellated form.
- **Altostratus (As)** – medium-level layer of cloud through which 'watery' sun may be seen.
- **Cirrus (Ci)** – high-level streaks of cloud formed by ice crystals, often referred to as 'mares' tails'.
- **Cirrocumulus (Cc)** – high-level heaped clouds which may assume regular rippled pattern (usually benign) of a 'mackerel sky'.
- **Cirrostratus (Cs)** – high-level layered cloud which may produce a 'halo' round the sun or moon.

Clouds are generally confined to the troposphere. This is the first 45,000 feet or so of the earth's atmosphere, within which the temperature falls as you go higher. Near the top of it, strong jet stream winds of 100 mph or more often blow in the direction a depression is moving, carrying the high-level clouds associated with it far ahead of the lower, heavier clouds that bring the rain. Cirrus clouds, therefore, are often a sign of approaching bad weather:

> *If clouds look as if scratched by a hen,*
> *Get ready to reef your topsails then.*

Such clouds are formed by showers of tiny ice crystals, which fall through the strong upper winds and appear to trail in one direction or another as their lateral movement slows down. The white streaks (the tips of the 'mares' tails') therefore point back towards the centre of low pressure advancing behind them. They also enable you to apply what is known as the **crossed wind rule**. This means that if you stand with your back to the surface wind and the clouds show that the upper wind is coming from your left, then the weather is probably deteriorating. This is related to '**Buys Ballots Law**' – if you stand with your

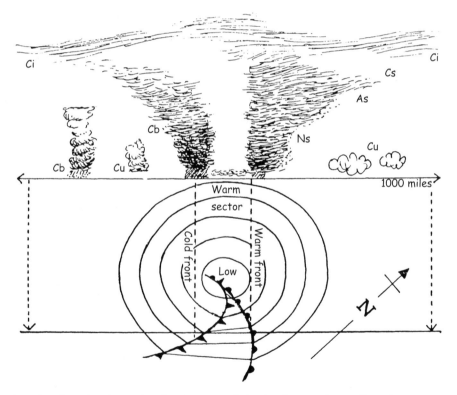

A section through a depression showing types of cloud and areas of rain. Most depressions are more complex than this, but the basic features can usually be recognised.

Estimated position

back to the wind (in the northern hemisphere) low pressure will be on your left.

Two other types of cloud that characterise a passing frontal depression are cirrostratus and cumulonimbus. In cirrostratus, the layered ice crystals often produce a warning halo effect round the sun or moon as a clear sky clouds over. In cumulonimbus, the tall clouds produce heavy rain showers as the unstable, blustery cold front comes through. However, by the time a complete low pressure system has come and gone, nearly all the cloud types will probably have been represented.

The shape of a depression

A large depression may easily be 1000 miles in extent, with cloud stretching 500 miles ahead of the warm front. Its speed of movement may be anything up to 60 knots – one of the hazards of weather forecasting – so you can see that it can take all day for the first warning cloud signs to be translated into the rain and turbulence of the frontal areas. Not that every depression produces rain, though. However, assuming a vigorous low, with two distinct frontal troughs in the classic form, the belt of rain along the warm front may be about 100 miles wide, and the cold front's rain belt perhaps 50 miles wide.

Two useful ways of visualising a depression

- Look down on the isobars of the familiar **weather map** and imagine two big swirls of cloud accompanying the fronts, as sometimes seen quite clearly on satellite pictures.
- Take a vertical **cross-section**, which is most usefully drawn (as in our illustration) along a SW–NE axis that cuts across the two fronts.

Now imagine the whole system tracking north-east. The map shows the shifting wind directions as felt by a more or less stationary yacht on the surface, the likely strength of the wind (**remember – the closer the isobars, the stronger the wind**), and the rise and fall of the barometer.

The cross-section shows the advancing warm front with the succession of cloud formations that precede it, the warm sector, and the wedge of cold air closing in behind it.

As the depression approaches, the wind will back southerly and the classic progression of clouds will probably appear: high wispy streaks of cloud (cirrus) spreading to shroud the sun (cirrostratus) and then steadily lowering and darkening (altostratus and nimbostratus) until the rain begins to fall – light at first, but soon settling into a continuous moderately heavy spell as the warm sector arrives. Meanwhile, the wind will have increased.

Entering the warm sector, fog or drizzle may reduce visibility even though the rain has eased. The temperature will rise (although the generally damp conditions will probably disguise this). The most significant effect for yachtsmen may well be the veering wind, which should then stay steady until the arrival of the cold front, when it will veer again towards the north-west, usually more sharply. The barometer will reflect the same pattern – steady, then rising rapidly.

If the low is a vigorous one, with steep pressure gradients (closely spaced isobars) and correspondingly strong winds (a fall in pressure of 5–6 millibars in three hours is considered 'rapid'), this is when they will be felt. The **cold front** is not only likely to bring heavy rain squalls, but its generally gusty winds will accentuate the cooler, fresher atmosphere. Towering thundery clouds may even produce some hail. At least a cold front tends to pass more quickly than its warm counterpart. The cloud sequence may now to some extent be reversed, but most important is the brisk process of heaped-up medium-level clouds (cumulus or cumulonimbus) with clear blue sky soon showing above.

On land it is a cheerful moment – the arrival of 'showers and bright periods' after a spell of miserable wet weather. At sea, it may mean pulling down the last reef and weathering the worst of the blow.

The anticyclone

For sailors, and those on land, **high pressure generally means fine weather**. The pressure gradients around an anticyclone are usually less steep than in a depression, so light winds are the rule and gales are a rarity. While the air continues to descend in the high, diverging outwards to feed the inward circulation of any neighbouring lows, it is compressed, warmed and dried. Moisture picked up from the cold sea may condense out, but at this low level the incipient cloud is often stifled by a temperature inversion – this is a layer of warm air sitting on top of the cooler surface air in which the cloud starts to form. Anticyclonic weather may therefore be dull and foggy, but it seldom rains.

Local weather

For the short time that most yachtsmen are at sea, local weather – such as sea breezes, violent squalls or fog – can be just as important as the big weather systems we have already mentioned.

Coastal **sea breezes** are produced in summer when rising air above the rapidly heated land surface sucks in air from offshore. These breezes reach

Flashing light (Fl) – dark period exceeds light

their peak on a hot afternoon, perhaps as much as force 4–5 (but not more), and die away at sunset. They are confined to within a few miles of the coastline, where a line of convective cumulus clouds over the land may indicate that such a breeze is developing. The first boat to pick this up could win the club handicap race by half a mile!

At night, when the land cools more rapidly than the sea (whose temperature scarcely changes) the reverse process may produce a **land breeze**, but it tends to be a weak affair by comparison. Where convection is more violent, round the base of a towering thunder cloud for example, the thermal up-draught can cause sudden **squalls** and localised wind shifts (if in any doubt, shorten sail quickly). The opposite sort of instability, when cold air rolls down the sides of a coastal valley or fjord, accentuating the night-time tendency to a land breeze, is called a **katabatic wind**.

For the racing yachtsman, the smallest of local effects – up-draughts, down-draughts, wind shadows, eddies in the lee of a headland, or the tendency for surface winds to back as they cross land – are worth anticipating. On the other hand, those cruising can sometimes pay too much anxious attention to weather forecasts. Unless you are in the Yachtmaster exam room, you only need be on the lookout for the few real dangers: a sudden deep low is one of them; fog in a crowded shipping lane is another.

Fog

The basic cause of fog, as we saw earlier, is air cooling to the critical temperature (the dew point) below which it can no longer hold all its moisture as invisible vapour. Surplus vapour then condenses out as water droplets suspended in the air. The resulting fog is given various names, depending on the circumstances. Frontal fog, for example, occurs where warm and cold air mix. But the two main types are **radiation or land fog**, and **advection or sea fog**.

Land fog occurs, generally in autumn and winter, when any warmth in the land is rapidly radiated into a clear sky so that the surface air is cooled below its dew point. A light breeze may help to diffuse the cooling effect and spread the fog – hence its importance to yachtsmen. It may drift out to sea for a few miles, particularly at dawn, when it is most prevalent.

Sea fog may also arrive from landward in the sense that warm air heated, for example, over the Continent, may release fog when it starts to move across the cool water of the North Sea. Fog in the Channel, especially in spring and early summer, may be brought by a warm, moist, south-westerly air stream blowing from the Azores across progressively colder seas. It is the critical relationship of temperatures and humidity that matters and, unfortunately for sailors, once the potential for fog exists, a rising wind may not blow it away. Sea fog can persist in force 5 or even 6. The right tactics for dealing with it (discussed later) are vital.

According to the wind indicator, it's easing.'

The Beaufort wind scale

Admiral Francis Beaufort's Scale of Wind Forces – what today we simply call the Beaufort scale – was originally defined in terms of the amount of sail a square rigged naval frigate could carry. Later it was used by fishing smacks. Now the scale is used both on land and sea, with various ways of describing the effect of specified wind speeds.

Experienced sailors today relate the wind force they hear about in a forecast to the effect it has on the boat or boats they are familiar with – just like Admiral Beaufort did. When left to make their own assessments, most people begin by exaggerating wind forces, but then the written descriptions are not necessarily that much help. We have included them here anyway – as seen on land as well as at sea – in case you find them of some use, perhaps while driving down to the boat and listening to the forecast on the radio.

Warm front

Beaufort scale

Force	Wind speed in knots	Forecast description	Wave height in metres	Sea state	Effects on land
0	<1	Calm	0	Like a mirror	Smoke rises vertically
1	1–3	Light	0	Ripples without crests	Smoke, but not vanes, indicate wind direction
2	4–6	Light	0.1	Small wavelets, but crests do not break	Leaves rustle; wind vanes move
3	7–10	Light	0.4	Large wavelets; crests begin to break	Wind extends light flag
4	11–16	Moderate	1	Small waves; fairly frequent white horses	Wind raises dust and loose paper; small branches move
5	17–21	Fresh	2	Moderate, longer waves; many white horses	Small trees in leaf begin to sway
6	22–27	Strong breeze	3	Large waves with foam crests; spray likely	Telegraph wires whistle; umbrellas difficult to use
7	28–33	Near gale	4	Foam streaks begin to appear	Whole trees in motion
8	34–40	Gale	5.5	Longer waves, well marked with foam streaks	Twigs break off; walking is difficult
9	41–47	Severe gale	7	High waves with dense streaks of foam, spray and tumbling crests	Slight structural damage, eg to chimney pots and slates
10	48–55	Storm	9	Very high waves with long overhanging crests and large patches of foam; tumbling crests are heavy; visibility is affected	Trees uprooted; considerable structural damage

Sources of weather information

Nearly all weather forecasts originate from the **Meteorological Office** (more usually referred to as the Met Office) at Exeter. The forecast office can be consulted directly by telephone, fax or internet; its *Marine Weather Services* booklet gives details. But most sailors use a variety of indirect sources – **BBC shipping forecasts, local radio** broadcasts, the **Marinecall** telephone service, **Navtex** (for which a special receiver is needed), **Coastguard** inshore forecasts, **television** and **newspapers**.

All of these have their different uses. Television forecasts, for example, are an excellent way to get a general picture of the weather before you set sail. The BBC in particular uses a thoroughly professional presentation; and some bulletins look several days ahead. A number of newspapers also publish proper weather maps that you can take aboard for reference, although they are inevitably based on yesterday's information. Coastguard stations provide a comprehensive service, but many sailors find their four-hourly inshore waters forecasts on VHF radio particularly convenient.

At the centre of all this information is the maritime ritual of the BBC shipping forecast, with its concise, coded language and repetitive sequence. If you want to draw your own weather map, this is your source. Using one of the RYA/R. Met. Soc. Metmaps will make this a lot easier. The Yachtmaster exam no longer requires such expertise, but an understanding of the shipping forecast remains an important part of the shorebased course.

The shipping forecast

The Met Office prepares the shipping forecast four times a day for broadcast by BBC Radio 4. At present this goes out at 0048, 0535, 1201 and 1754. The first two of these broadcasts are followed by a supplementary forecast for the inshore waters of the UK, divided into nine areas.

The main shipping forecast consists of four elements:

- **Gale warnings** – a summary of any warnings in force.
- **A general synopsis**.
- **Area forecasts**.
- **Reports from coastal stations** (0048 and 0535 only).

The **synopsis** gives the position of the main depressions, anticyclones, troughs and fronts from the latest analysis by the central forecast office (that is, about 6 hours previously), the central pressure of the lows and highs, and their expected movement over the next 24 hours – a deep low off southern Ireland, for example,

Direction of buoyage

might be expected to reach the North Sea by the same time on the following day. The sea **area forecasts** come next, always in the same order, starting with Viking, off Norway, then clockwise round the British Isles through Humber and Thames, Wight and Portland, Rockall and Malin, to finish in south-east Iceland. (Note that after lengthy negotiations with the French and Spanish weathermen, sea area Finisterre has recently been renamed FitzRoy and given a slightly different boundary.) For each area, details are given of changing wind, weather and visibility for the next 24 hours.

The five-minute bulletin ends twice a day with **reports from coastal stations** in a similar clockwise sequence – currently Tiree, Stornaway, Lerwick, Fife Ness, Bridlington, Sandettie light vessel, Greenwich light vessel, Jersey, Channel light vessel, Scilly, Valentia, Ronaldsway and Malin Head – describing the local wind direction and force, the weather, the visibility in miles or metres, the atmos-

'What does it mean when the shipping forecast is interrupted by Prayer for the Day?'

pheric pressure in millibars, and how it is changing. Some of these weather stations, including the light vessels, are entirely automatic, with clever equipment for deducing from the local atmosphere how far a human being could see, as well as measuring wind and pressure.

The language of these forecasts is precise and economical. It forms a mesmeric pattern – fascinating even to non-sailors who have not the slightest practical interest in whether it is blowing a north-westerly gale on the Dogger Bank! Superfluous words like 'wind force' and 'visibility' are omitted, while each of those included has a careful definition. **Gale warnings** will be given if mean wind speeds of force 8 (34–40 knots) or gusts of more than 43 knots are expected; a gale is 'imminent' if it arrives within 6 hours; 'moderate' visibility is 2–5 miles.

When giving the forecast for sea area Dover, for example, the BBC announcer may simply say: 'Northwesterly 5, Fair, Good', meaning that the wind will blow from the north-west at force 5 (17–21 knots), the weather will be fair (that is, no rain showers, mist or fog), and the visibility good (more than 5 miles). The definitions may seem arbitrary, but they should be learned thoroughly, both to understand the forecast – and because they may be the subject of specific questions in the meteorology assessment paper.

Terminology in shipping forecasts

Gale warnings and timing
- **Gales** – mean wind speeds of F8 (34–40 knots) or gusts of more than 43 knots.
- **Severe gales** – mean wind speed of F9 (41–47 knots) or gusts of more than 51 knots.
- **Storm** – mean wind speed of F10 (48–55 knots) or gusts of more than 60 knots.
- **Imminent** – within 6 hours.
- **Soon** – in 6 to 12 hours.
- **Later** – in more than 12 hours.

Movement of pressure systems
- **Slowly** – up to 15 knots.
- **Steadily** – 15 to 25 knots.
- **Rather quickly** – 25 to 35 knots.
- **Rapidly** – 35 to 45 knots.
- **Very rapidly** – more than 45 knots.

Pressure tendency (change in previous three hours)
- **Steady** – less than 0.1 millibars.
- **Rising (or) falling slowly** – 0.1 to 1.5 millibars.
- **Rising (or) falling** – 1.6 to 3.5 millibars.

- **Rising (or) falling quickly** – 3.6 to 6.0 millibars.
- **Rising (or) falling very rapidly** – more than 6.0 millibars.
- **Now falling or now rising** – direction of change reversed.

Visibility
- **Good** – more than 5 nautical miles.
- **Moderate** – 2 to 5 nautical miles.
- **Poor** – 1000 metres to 2 nautical miles.
- **Fog** – less than 1000 metres.

Position of fog symbol

To take all this information down and create your **own weather map** (an exercise that is not currently part of the Yachtmaster course) really requires the kind of forms and charts published by the RYA and the Met Office for this purpose, with the sequence of sea areas listed and marked. The charts may have scales for converting spacing of isobars into wind forces or knots (a cold front's pressure gradient produces relatively stronger winds than a warm one).

You will also need some sort of shorthand, however informal. Meteorologists have their own international plotting symbols, but there is also a simple **Beaufort notation**, using single letters (which apart from p for showers) are almost self-evident: **rain – r; drizzle – d; snow – s; showers – p; hail – h; thunder – t; squalls – q; mist – m; fog – f; haze – z; calm – o.** Wind directions and forces taken down as letters and numbers can be transferred to the chart with small half-feathered arrows .

But it matters little what symbols you use as long as they are intelligible and quick to record. The single letters L and H are obvious for low and high. A horizontal arrow can show that something – perhaps a wind direction and force – is 'becoming' something else; an oblique line will indicate the forecaster's habitual distinction between the situation 'at first' and 'later'. Coastal reports are easier to deal with than area forecasts because the pattern is clearly fixed, but you still have to move fast. Just the last two numbers will do for pressures. And in the last column, show the pressure tendency with a line – a horizontal one for 'steady', a sloping one for 'falling', and so on.

When you start drawing the isobars on the chart, do not expect them to produce the clear bold pattern found in textbook illustrations. Taken from a real shipping forecast, they can be maddeningly ambiguous.

Points to remember about weather forecasting

- Concentrate on recording the essential elements of the general synopsis, even if you miss some of the area forecasts.
- If you get behind with the coastal reports, give priority to wind directions and pressures; these will help draw the first few isobars.
- Do not miss your own sea area while worrying about the others!

Safety and Seagoing Practice

The Rule of the Road

You don't need to be a sailor to know that ships carry a green navigation light on their starboard side and a red one to port, or that steam traditionally gives way to sail. Hire a motor cruiser on the Thames and the boatman will probably explain that in a narrow channel it is customary to 'drive on the right'.

Such basic principles were evolved as part of what maritime lawyers call 'the ordinary practice of seamen'. But nowadays they are codified, along with many more complex rules, in the *International Regulations for Preventing Collisions at Sea* – called the **colregs** for short. They are drafted by a London-based organisation known as the International Maritime Organisation (IMO), whose members include all the major maritime flag states.

The current regulations date from 1972, although they have been amended several times since, most recently in 2001. The fundamental principle of steam giving way to sail has survived, but only just. It is severely constrained by other rules that give priority to large commercial craft.

The regulations come in **four parts**:

A – **general rules and definitions**
B – **steering and sailing rules**
C – **lights and shapes**
D – **sound and light signals**

Most of these rules are of great practical importance at sea, whether you command a 5-ton yacht or a 50,000-ton tanker, and they form a correspondingly large part of the Yachtmaster course. We have therefore presented them almost in their entirety. But to make this large chunk digestible, we have included explanatory notes, occasional summaries, and a **variety of typefaces for different sorts of information**.

Starboard hand buoy

- The TEXT IN CAPITALS indicates KEY PHRASES, or in some cases complete rules, that may be worth skimming through *just* before the examination. Some of these are simply definitions; others are important because they convey in carefully drafted legal language some rule that would otherwise be ambiguous. The obligations of the 'stand-on' vessel in a crossing situation are a good example. Another rule of great significance to yachtsmen (because they have been heavily fined for disregarding it) states that vessels crossing traffic separation lanes shall do so 'as nearly as practicable at right angles to the general direction of traffic flow'. The essential text in capitals comprises about 1600 words, so it should take no more than 10–15 minutes to read right through.
- Less important sections of the rules are summarised here in square brackets – eg [rules apply in any visibility].
- *Text set in italic* denotes rules that are of *direct or special relevance to yachtsmen*. The steering rules for sailing vessels obviously come into this category – starboard tack has right of way, and so on – as do the navigation lights that must be carried by yachts.

- Explanatory notes and comments by the authors are tinted.

International Regulations for Preventing Collisions at Sea, 1972

Part A – General Rules and Definitions

Examiners can show a surprising predeliction for broad questions of definition, or tricky ones of the 'When is a door not a door?' variety! For that reason, this first section is worth more attention than you might otherwise give it.

Rule 1 – Application

a) These RULES shall APPLY TO ALL VESSELS UPON THE HIGH SEAS and in all waters connected therewith navigable by seagoing vessels.
b) Nothing in these rules shall interfere with the operation of special rules made by an appropriate authority for roadsteads, harbours, rivers, lakes or inland waterways . . .
c) [governments can make special rules for warships and fishing fleets]

Beats me why they operate harbour signals for small boats like that.'

Rule 2 – Responsibility

a) Nothing in these rules shall exonerate any vessel or the owner, master or crew thereof, from the consequences of any neglect to comply with these rules or of the neglect of any precaution which may be required by the ordinary practice of seamen, or by the special circumstances of the case.

b) In construing and complying with these rules due regard shall be had to all dangers of navigation and collision and to any special circumstances, including the limitations of the vessels involved, which may make a departure from these rules necessary to avoid immediate danger.

In other words, pedantic adherence to the written rules is not enough, either at sea or in the courtroom.

Rule 3 – General definitions

For the purpose of these rules, except where the context otherwise requires:

a) The word 'VESSEL' includes EVERY DESCRIPTION OF WATER CRAFT, including non-displacement craft and seaplanes . . .

b) The term 'POWER-DRIVEN VESSEL' means any vessel PROPELLED BY MACHINERY.

c) *The term 'SAILING VESSEL' means any vessel UNDER SAIL PROVIDED THAT PROPELLING MACHINERY, IF FITTED, IS NOT BEING USED.*

Beaufort 8 – gale

With her auxiliary engine switched on, a sailing yacht becomes a powerboat.

d) The term 'VESSEL ENGAGED IN FISHING' means any vessel fishing WITH NETS, LINES, TRAWLS OR OTHER FISHING APPARATUS WHICH RESTRICT MANOEUVRABILITY . . .
e) [definition of a seaplane]
f) The term 'VESSEL NOT UNDER COMMAND' means a vessel which THROUGH SOME EXCEPTIONAL CIRCUMSTANCES is UNABLE TO MANOEUVRE AS REQUIRED BY THESE RULES and is therefore unable to keep out of the way of another vessel.
g) The term 'RESTRICTED IN HER ABILITY TO MANOEUVRE' means a vessel which FROM THE NATURE OF HER WORK IS RESTRICTED in her ability to manoeuvre as required by these rules and is therefore unable to keep out of the way of another vessel. [there follows a series of examples of such vessels, including cable layers, dredgers, buoy tenders, survey ships, tugs engaged in towing, and warships minesweeping or launching aircraft]
h) The term 'VESSEL CONSTRAINED BY HER DRAFT' means a power-driven vessel which, because of her draught in relation to the available depth and width of navigable water, is SEVERELY RESTRICTED IN HER ABILITY TO DEVIATE from the course she is following.
i) The term 'UNDER WAY' means that a vessel is NOT AT ANCHOR, OR MADE FAST TO THE SHORE, OR AGROUND.

Note that 'under way' is not the same as 'making way through the water'.

j) [definition of dimensions]
k) Vessels shall be deemed to be in sight of one another only when one can be observed visually from the other.

Radar does not count as 'seeing'.

l) The term 'RESTRICTED VISIBILITY' means any conditions in which visibility is restricted by FOG, MIST, FALLING SNOW, HEAVY RAINSTORMS, SANDSTORMS or any other similar causes.

PART B – Steering and Sailing Rules
Section 1 – Conduct of vessels in any condition of visibility

Some more definitions; a lot of good practical advice such as the need to make bold, early changes of course when avoiding collision; and the important Rule 10 on traffic separation schemes – its key message being that a small yacht must not 'impede the passage' of large commercial craft through such crowded waters.

Rule 4 – [rules apply in any visibility]

Rule 5 – Look-out

Every vessel shall at all times maintain a proper look-out by sight and hearing as well as by all available means appropriate in the prevailing circumstances and conditions so as to make a full appraisal of the situation and the risk of collision.

Fine sentiments, but remember they are no guarantee that a large ship will notice a small yacht under her bows.

Rule 6 – Safe speed

Every vessel shall at all times proceed at a safe speed so that she can take proper and effective action to avoid collision and be stopped within a distance appropriate to the prevailing circumstances and conditions.

In other words, in a seamanlike manner.

In determining a safe speed the following factors shall be among those taken into account:
a) By all vessels:
   (i)   the state of visibility
   (ii)   the traffic density including concentrations of fishing vessels . . .
   (iii) the manoeuvrability of the vessel with special reference to stopping distance and turning ability . . .
   (iv)   at night the presence of background light such as from shore lights . . .
   (v)   the state of wind, sea and current, and the proximity of navigational hazards
   (vi)   the draught in relation to the available depth of water.

Transferred position line

b) Additionally, by vessels with operational radar:
  (i)   the characteristics, efficiency and limitations of the radar equipment [five more sub-sections elaborating on (i)].

Rule 7 – Risk of collision

a) Every vessel shall use all available means appropriate to the prevailing circumstances and conditions to determine if risk of collision exists. If there is any doubt, such risk shall be deemed to exist.
b) Proper use shall be made of radar equipment if fitted and operational, including long-range scanning to obtain early warning of risk of collision and radar plotting or equivalent systematic observation of detected objects.

To avoid the notorious 'radar-assisted' collision.

c) Assumptions shall not be made on the basis of scanty information, especially scanty radar information.
d) In determining if risk of collision exists, the following considerations shall be among those taken into account:
  (i)   SUCH RISK shall be deemed to exist IF THE COMPASS BEARING OF AN APPROACHING VESSEL DOES NOT APPRECIABLY CHANGE.

A basic working rule, not just a legal precept.

  (ii) such risk may sometimes exist even when an appreciable bearing change is evident, particularly when approaching a very large vessel, or a tow, or when approaching a vessel at close range.

Rule 8 – Action to avoid collision

a) Any ACTION TO AVOID COLLISION shall, if the circumstances of the case admit, be POSITIVE, made IN AMPLE TIME and with due regard to the observance of good seamanship.
b) ANY ALTERATION OF COURSE AND/OR SPEED to avoid collision shall, if the circumstances of the case permit, be LARGE ENOUGH TO BE READILY APPARENT TO ANOTHER VESSEL OBSERVING VISUALLY OR BY RADAR; a succession of small alterations of course and/or speed should be avoided.

Points a) and b) offer excellent practical advice, especially when approaching large ships.

c) If there is sufficient sea room, alteration of course alone may be the most effective action to avoid a close-quarters situation provided that it is made in good time, is substantial, and does not result in another close-quarters situation.

d) Action to avoid collision with another vessel shall be such as to result in passing at a safe distance . . .

e) If necessary to avoid collision or allow more time to assess the situation, a vessel shall slacken her speed or take all way off . . .

f) [this rule does not contradict rules about 'not impeding passage']

Rule 9 – Narrow channels

a) A VESSEL proceeding along the course of a narrow channel or fairway SHALL KEEP as near TO THE OUTER LIMIT OF THE CHANNEL OR FAIRWAY WHICH LIES ON HER STARBOARD SIDE as is safe and practicable.

b) *A vessel of less than 20 metres in length or a SAILING VESSEL SHALL NOT IMPEDE THE PASSAGE OF A VESSEL WHICH CAN SAFELY NAVIGATE ONLY WITHIN A NARROW CHANNEL or fairway.*

c) A VESSEL ENGAGED IN FISHING SHALL NOT IMPEDE THE PASSAGE of any other vessel navigating within a narrow channel or fairway.

d) A VESSEL SHALL NOT CROSS A NARROW CHANNEL OR FAIRWAY IF SUCH CROSSING IMPEDES the passage of a vessel which can safely navigate only within such channel or fairway. The latter vessel may use the sound signal prescribed in **Rule 34d**

(Five short and rapid blasts.)

if in doubt as to the intention of the crossing vessel.

e) (i)   In a narrow channel or fairway when overtaking can take place only if the vessel to be overtaken takes action to permit safe passing, the VESSEL INTENDING TO OVERTAKE shall indicate her intention by SOUNDING THE APPROPRIATE SIGNAL prescribed in **Rule 34c (i)**

(Two long blasts and one short blast if overtaking to starboard; two long and two short to port.)

The VESSEL TO BE OVERTAKEN shall, IF IN AGREEMENT, SOUND THE APPROPRIATE SIGNAL prescribed in **Rule 34c (ii)**

(Long, short, long, short blasts.)

and take steps to permit safe passing. IF IN DOUBT she MAY SOUND THE SIGNALS prescribed in **Rule 34d**

(Five short and rapid blasts.)

(ii)   [**Rule 13** still applies, ie keep clear when overtaking]

Overfalls, tide rips, races

f) A VESSEL NEARING A BEND or an area of a narrow channel or fairway where other vessels may be obscured by an intervening obstruction shall navigate with particular alertness and caution and shall SOUND THE APPROPRIATE SIGNAL prescribed in **Rule 34e**

(One long blast.)

g) ANY VESSEL shall, if the circumstances of the case admit, AVOID ANCHORING IN A NARROW CHANNEL.

Rule 10 – Traffic separation schemes

a) This rule applies to traffic separation schemes adopted by IMO and does not relieve any vessel of her obligation under any other rule.
b) A VESSEL USING A TRAFFIC SCHEME shall:
   (i)   PROCEED in the appropriate traffic lane IN THE GENERAL DIRECTION OF TRAFFIC for that lane;
   (ii) so far as practicable KEEP CLEAR OF a traffic separation line or SEPARATION ZONE;
   (iii) NORMALLY JOIN OR LEAVE A TRAFFIC LANE AT THE TERMINATION of the lane . . .
c) A VESSEL SHALL so far as practicable avoid crossing traffic lanes, but if obliged to do so, shall CROSS ON A HEADING AS NEARLY AS PRACTICABLE AT RIGHT ANGLES TO THE GENERAL DIRECTION OF TRAFFIC FLOW.

This is obviously a particularly important rule for yachts crossing the English Channel. Its purpose is to minimise the time spent in the traffic lanes by steering straight across instead of heading up-tide to make good a right-angled course. Coastguards watching on radar will, or should, allow for this. The phrase 'as nearly as practicable' also covers a yacht's inability to sail straight into the wind.

d) Inshore traffic zones shall not normally be used by through traffic which can safely use the appropriate traffic lane within the adjacent traffic separation scheme. However *VESSELS OF LESS THAN 20 METRES IN LENGTH AND SAILING VESSELS MAY UNDER ALL CIRCUMSTANCES USE INSHORE TRAFFIC ZONES.*
e) A VESSEL OTHER THAN A CROSSING VESSEL or a vessel joining or leaving a lane shall NOT NORMALLY ENTER A SEPARATION ZONE or cross a separation line EXCEPT: in case of EMERGENCY to avoid immediate danger; to engage in FISHING within a separation zone.
f) [take care near the end of traffic schemes]
g) [avoid anchoring in or near schemes]
h) [give schemes a wide berth]

'I always play safe and go astern of them.'

i) [fishing vessels must not impede vessels using schemes]

j) *A VESSEL OF LESS THAN 20 METRES OR A SAILING VESSEL shall NOT IMPEDE THE SAFE PASSAGE OF A POWER-DRIVEN VESSEL FOLLOWING A TRAFFIC LANE.*

k) [scheme maintenance vessels may be exempt from this rule]

l) [cable layers may be exempt from this rule]

Section 2 – Conduct of vessels in sight of one another

Rule 11 – *[this section covers vessels in sight of one another]*

Rule 12 – *Sailing vessels*

a) *When two sailing vessels are approaching one another so as to involve the risk of collision, one of them shall keep out of the way of the other as follows:*

(i) *when each has the WIND ON A DIFFERENT SIDE, the vessel which has the wind on the PORT SIDE SHALL KEEP OUT OF THE WAY of the other;*

(ii) *when both have the WIND ON THE SAME SIDE, the vessel which is to WINDWARD SHALL KEEP OUT OF THE WAY of the vessel which is to leeward;*

(iii) *if a vessel with the wind on the port side sees a vessel to windward and CANNOT DETERMINE WITH CERTAINTY whether the other vessel has the wind on the port or the starboard side, she shall KEEP OUT OF THE WAY of the other.*

Isolated danger mark

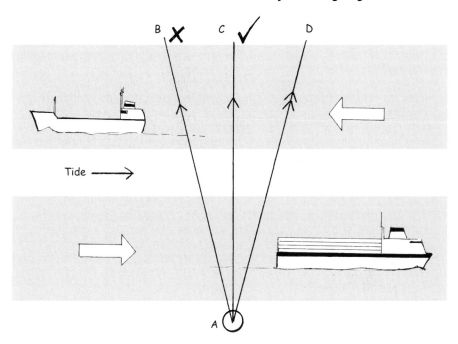

Crossing shipping lanes. Normally, to arrive at C, a yachtsman would steer course AB to allow for the tide. The correct procedure, however, is to steer AC and, because of the tidal set, arrive at D.

b) *For the purposes of this rule the WINDWARD SIDE shall be deemed to be the side OPPOSITE TO that on which the MAINSAIL is carried or, in the case of a square-rigged vessel, the side opposite to that on which the largest fore-and-aft sail is carried.*

Summary – starboard tack has right of way; on same tack, windward boat gives way; if in doubt, keep clear.

Rule 13 – Overtaking

a) Notwithstanding anything contained in the rules ANY VESSEL OVERTAKING any other shall KEEP OUT OF THE WAY of the vessel being overtaken.

b) A vessel shall be deemed to be OVERTAKING WHEN coming up with another vessel FROM A DIRECTION MORE THAN 22.5° ABAFT HER BEAM, that is, in such a position with reference to the vessel she is overtaking that AT NIGHT she would be able to SEE ONLY THE STERNLIGHT of that vessel, but neither of her sidelights.

c) When a vessel is in doubt as to whether she is overtaking another, she shall assume that this is the case, and act accordingly.

Note the general principle, also applied in Rules 12 and 14, that if in doubt you keep clear.

d) Any subsequent alteration of the bearing between the two vessels shall not make the overtaking vessel a crossing vessel within the meaning of these rules, or relieve her of the duty of keeping clear of the overtaken vessel until she is finally past and clear.

The disastrous collision off the Isle of Wight in 1970 between the tankers *Pacific Glory* and *Allegro* involved the potential conflict – referred to here – between Rule 13 and the crossing rule, Rule 15.

Rule 14 – Head-on situation

a) When TWO POWER-DRIVEN VESSELS are MEETING ON RECIPROCAL OR NEARLY RECIPROCAL COURSES so as to involve the risk of collision EACH SHALL ALTER HER COURSE TO STARBOARD so that each shall pass on the port side of the other.

b) Such a situation shall be deemed to exist when a vessel sees the other ahead or nearly ahead and by night she can see the masthead lights of the other in line or nearly in line and/or both sidelights, and by day she observes the corresponding aspect of the other vessel.

c) When a vessel is in any doubt as to whether such a situation exists, she shall assume that it does and act accordingly.

Generations of sailors have learnt this rule by memorising Thomas Gray's verses:

When you see three lights ahead,
Starboard wheel and show your Red,
Green to Green or Red to Red,
Perfect safety, go ahead.

Rule 15 – Crossing situation

When TWO POWER-DRIVEN VESSELS are CROSSING so as to involve risk of collision, the VESSEL WHICH HAS THE OTHER ON HER OWN STARBOARD SIDE SHALL KEEP OUT OF THE WAY and shall, if the circumstances of the case admit, avoid crossing ahead of the other vessel.

Lighted offshore platform

The Thomas Gray version goes like this:

If to your starboard Red appear,
It is your duty to keep clear,
But when upon your port is seen
A steamer's starboard light of Green,
There's not so much for you to do;
The green light must keep clear of you.

'I'll be glad to get in, I've had enough excitement for one day.'

Rule 16 – Action by give-way vessel

Every vessel which is directed to keep out of the way of another vessel shall, so far as possible, take early and substantial action to keep well clear.

Note the 'early and substantial'

Rule 17 - Action by stand-on-vessel

a) (i)   WHERE ONE of two vessels IS TO KEEP OUT OF THE WAY, THE OTHER SHALL KEEP HER COURSE AND SPEED.

(ii)   The LATTER MAY HOWEVER TAKE ACTION to avoid collision BY HER MANOEUVRE ALONE AS SOON AS it becomes apparent to her that the VESSEL REQUIRED TO KEEP OUT OF THE WAY IS NOT TAKING APPROPRIATE ACTION in compliance with these rules.

b) When, from any cause, the vessel required to keep her course and speed finds herself so close that collision cannot be avoided by the action of the give-way vessel alone, she shall take such action as will best aid to avoid collision.

The careful legal wording of a) and b), though perhaps confusing, is vital in some collision situations between large vessels. Small yachts should try to apply the more basic rules of self-preservation.

c) A POWER-DRIVEN VESSEL WHICH TAKES ACTION IN A CROSSING SITUATION in accordance with sub-paragraph a) (ii) of this rule to avoid collision with another power-driven vessel SHALL, if the circumstances of the case permit, NOT ALTER COURSE TO PORT FOR A VESSEL ON HER OWN PORT SIDE.
d) This rule does not relieve the give-way vessel of her obligation to keep out of the way.

Rule 18 – Responsibilities between vessels

The following marine hierarchy, or 'pecking order', is obvious exam material, and worth learning. Once again, remember that an auxiliary sailing yacht is a 'power-driven vessel' when her engine is being used.

Except where **Rules 9, 10** and 13 otherwise require –
a) A POWER-DRIVEN VESSEL under way shall KEEP OUT OF THE WAY OF:
(i)   A VESSEL NOT UNDER COMMAND;
(ii)   A VESSEL RESTRICTED IN HER ABILITY TO MANOEUVRE;
(iii) A VESSEL ENGAGED IN FISHING;
(iv)   A SAILING VESSEL.
b) *A SAILING VESSEL under way shall keep out of the way of:*
(i)   *A VESSEL NOT UNDER COMMAND;*
(ii)   *A VESSEL RESTRICTED IN HER ABILITY TO MANOEUVRE;*
(iii) *A VESSEL ENGAGED IN FISHING.*
c) A VESSEL ENGAGED IN FISHING when under way shall, so far as possible, keep out of the way of:
(i)   A VESSEL NOT UNDER COMMAND;
(ii)   A VESSEL RESTRICTED IN HER ABILITY TO MANOEUVRE.
d) (i)   ANY VESSEL OTHER THAN A VESSEL NOT UNDER COMMAND OR A VESSEL RESTRICTED IN HER ABILITY TO MANOEUVRE shall, if the circumstances of the case admit, AVOID IMPEDING THE SAFE PASSAGE of a VESSEL CONSTRAINED BY HER DRAUGHT, exhibiting the signals in **Rule 28**

Wreck: not dangerous

Three vertical all-round reds or a cylinder.

(ii)   [a vessel constrained by her draught should take special care]
e) [seaplanes should keep well clear]

The maritime 'pecking order'

Vessel Not Under Command
Vessel Restricted in her Ability to Manoeuvre
Vessel Constrained by her Draught
Fishing Vessel – provided she is actually engaged in fishing
Sailing Vessel – but she loses this status when using an auxiliary engine
Power-driven Vessel – she gains status when following a traffic separation lane
Seaplane – definitely bottom of the pile

Modern commercial ships are often big, clumsy and fast. They can be upon you from over the horizon in less than 10 minutes; they may need 5 or 6 miles to stop; they can rarely take quick avoiding action. In reality, therefore, the seafaring status of a small sailing yacht is less than the colregs would suggest. She should stay clear of her big sisters whenever possible, especially in crowded waters and harbour entrances, and she should definitely not rely on the tradition of steam giving way to sail.

Section 3 – Conduct of vessels in restricted visibility

This is a section of the rules not always fully observed, and one where the relatively privileged legal position still enjoyed by small sailing craft is more than usually artificial.

Rule 19

a) [applies to vessels that cannot see one another]
b) EVERY VESSEL SHALL PROCEED AT A SAFE SPEED ADAPTED TO THE PRE-VAILING CIRCUMSTANCES and conditions of restricted visibility. A power-driven vessel shall have her engines ready for immediate manoeuvre.

Flag V   ● ● ● ▬

c) [take account of poor visibility when following other rules]

d) A vessel which detects by radar alone the presence of another vessel shall determine if a close-quarters situation is developing and/or risk of collision exists. If so, she shall take avoiding action in ample time, provided that when such action consists of an alteration of course, so far as possible the following shall be avoided:

   (i)   an alteration of course to port for a vessel forward of the beam, other than for a vessel being overtaken;

   (ii)   an alteration of course towards a vessel abeam or abaft the beam.

e) Except where it has been determined that a risk of collision does not exist, every vessel which hears apparently forward of her beam the fog signal of another vessel, or which cannot avoid a close-quarters situation with another vessel forward of her beam, shall reduce her speed to the minimum at which she can be kept on her course. She shall if necessary take all her way off and in any event navigate with extreme caution until danger of collision is over.

PART C – Lights and shapes

Laid out merely as a mass of overlapping regulations, the rules on lights and shapes can look dreadfully confusing. But by logical grouping and elimination – which we have tried to apply in the illustrations – they can be made more manageable. After all, every one of them, from the multi-coloured array that makes a dredger look like a floating Christmas tree, to a small sailing boat's solitary white light, is designed to convey information.

Of the four colours in the basic rules, one can quickly be disposed of because it so rarely occurs. A steady yellow light is confined to tugs, shown above the sternlight to indicate that the vessel is towing. A hover-craft has a flashing yellow light, and a vessel fishing with a seine net may show a pair of alternately flashing yellow lights if she is hampered by her gear. Apart from these few cases – and the lifeboat's blue flashing light – we are dealing with combinations of white, red and green.

The first distinction to be made here is between directional lights that are meant to convey a perspective of movement through the darkness, and all-round lights which generally tell you what sort of vessel you are looking at. A large ship's basic navigation lights, for example, consist of red and green sidelights and a pair of forward-facing white masthead lights, with the rear one set higher than the other so you can tell instantly which way she is heading. But the additional green and white lights shown by a fishing trawler – whether or not she is moving – are visible all round. So are the white and red lights carried by a pilot vessel (same colours as the pilot flag H) or the two reds of a vessel not under command.

The colour red, you will notice, is generally associated with situations of difficulty or danger – vessels aground, manoeuvring with difficulty, constrained by their draught, and so on.

Another principle running through the IMO system is that you add lights as the vessel – or combination of vessels – gets larger. A small tug on her own may show just a single masthead light, for instance. A tug more than 50 metres long must carry a second, similar light aft. When towing, the forward light is doubled up, and if the length of the tow exceeds 200 metres, she adds a third. Seen from dead ahead, therefore, she will by now present a vertical line of four white lights, plus the red and green sidelights to port and starboard.

Rule 21 – Definitions

a) 'MASTHEAD LIGHT' – [white light over arc of 225° FROM RIGHT AHEAD TO 22.5° ABAFT THE BEAM on each side]
b) 'SIDELIGHTS' – [red to port, green to starboard, in each case over ARC OF 112.5° FROM RIGHT AHEAD TO 22.5° ABAFT THE BEAM; but in *VESSEL LESS THAN 20 METRES LONG SIDELIGHTS MAY BE COMBINED IN ONE LANTERN on centreline*]
c) 'STERNLIGHT' – [CENTRED AFT TO SHOW OVER ARC OF 135° NOT COVERED BY MASTHEAD AND SIDELIGHTS]
d) 'Towing light' – [same as sternlight but yellow]

Rule 22 – Visibility of lights

a) Vessels of 50 metres or more in length: masthead 6 miles; others 3 miles.
b) Vessels of 12–50 metres: masthead 5 miles (3 miles if less than 20 metres long); others 2 miles.
c) *Vessels of less than 12 metres: masthead/sternlight/towing light/all-round light 2 miles; sidelight 1 mile.*

Rule 23 – Power-driven vessels under way

a) A POWER-DRIVEN VESSEL UNDER WAY shall exhibit:
  (i)   a MASTHEAD LIGHT forward;
  (ii) a SECOND MASTHEAD LIGHT abaft of and higher than the forward one *(except that a VESSEL OF LESS THAN 50 METRES in length SHALL NOT BE OBLIGED TO exhibit such light, but may do so)*;

(iii)   SIDELIGHTS;

(iv)   a STERNLIGHT.

b) An AIR-CUSHION VESSEL when operating in the non-displacement mode shall, in addition to the lights prescribed in paragraph a) of this rule, exhibit an ALL-ROUND FLASHING LIGHT.

c) (i)   *A POWER-DRIVEN VESSEL OF LESS THAN 12 METRES in length may in lieu of the lights prescribed in paragraph a) of this rule exhibit an ALL-ROUND WHITE LIGHT AND SIDELIGHTS.*

(ii)   *A POWER-DRIVEN VESSEL OF LESS THAN 7 METRES in length whose maximum speed does not exceed 7 knots may in lieu of the lights pre scribed in paragraph a) of this rule exhibit an ALL-ROUND WHITE LIGHT and shall, if practicable, also exhibit sidelights.*

Rule 24 – Towing and pushing

a) A POWER-DRIVEN VESSEL WHEN TOWING shall exhibit:

(i)   instead of the light prescribed in **Rule 23a (i)**

The forward masthead light,

TWO MASTHEAD LIGHTS FORWARD in a vertical line; WHEN THE LENGTH OF THE TOW,measuring from the stern of the towing vessel to the after end of the tow, EXCEEDS 200 METRES, THREE SUCH LIGHTS in a vertical line;

(ii)   SIDELIGHTS;

(iii)   a STERNLIGHT;

(iv)   a TOWING LIGHT in a vertical line ABOVE THE STERNLIGHT;

(v)   WHEN THE LENGTH OF THE TOW EXCEEDS 200 METRES, A DIAMOND SHAPE (by day) where it can best be seen.

In other words, the characteristics of a tug towing at night are the extra white masthead lights when seen from ahead and, usually, the yellow towing light seen from astern.

b) When a pushing vessel and a vessel being pushed ahead are rigidly connected in a composite unit they shall be regarded as a power-driven vessel and exhibit the lights prescribed in **Rule 23**.

c) A POWER-DRIVEN VESSEL WHEN PUSHING AHEAD OR TOWING ALONGSIDE, except in the case of a composite unit, shall exhibit:

(i)   instead of the light prescribed in **Rule 23a (i)**

The forward masthead light),

TWO MASTHEAD LIGHTS FORWARD in a vertical line;

(ii)   SIDELIGHTS;

West cardinal buoy

(iii)   a STERNLIGHT.

Note the absence of the yellow towing light in this situation.

d) A power-driven vessel to which paragraphs a) or c) of this rule apply shall also comply with **Rule 23a (ii)**

Covering the second masthead light aft in larger vessels.

e) A VESSEL OR OBJECT BEING TOWED, other than those mentioned in paragraph g) of the rule

(ie semi-submerged),

shall exhibit:
(i)   SIDELIGHTS;
(ii)   a STERNLIGHT;
(iii)   when the length of the tow exceeds 200 metres, a diamond shape where it can best be seen.
f) Provided that any number of vessels being towed alongside or pushed in a group shall be lighted as one vessel: a vessel being pushed ahead, not being part of a composite unit, shall exhibit at the forward end, sidelights; a vessel being towed alongside shall exhibit a sternlight and at the forward end, sidelights.
g) An inconspicuous partly submerged vessel or object, or combination of such vessels or objects being towed, shall exhibit... [multiple all-round white lights and diamonds to indicate their size].
h) Where from any sufficient cause it is impracticable for a vessel or object being towed to exhibit the lights or shapes prescribed in paragraphs e) or g) of this rule, all possible measures shall be taken to light the vessel or object towed or at least to indicate its presence

(eg using a searchlight to illuminate the tow).

Rule 25 – Sailing vessels under way and vessels under oars
a) *A SAILING VESSEL UNDER WAY shall exhibit:*
(i)   *SIDELIGHTS;*
(ii)   *a STERNLIGHT;*
b) *In a SAILING VESSEL OF LESS THAN 12 METRES in length the LIGHTS prescribed in paragraph a) of this rule MAY BE COMBINED IN ONE LANTERN carried at or near the top of the mast where it can best be seen.*
c) *A SAILING VESSEL under way may, IN ADDITION to the lights prescribed in*

paragraph a) of this rule, exhibit at or near the top of the mast, where they can best be seen, TWO ALL-ROUND LIGHTS in a vertical line, THE UPPER BEING RED AND THE LOWER GREEN, but these lights shall not be exhibited in conjunction with the combined lantern permitted by paragraph b) of this rule.

d) *A SAILING VESSEL OF LESS THAN 7 METRES in length shall, if practicable, exhibit the lights prescribed in paragraph a) or b) of this rule, but if she does not, she shall have ready at hand AN ELECTRIC TORCH OR LIGHTED LANTERN showing a white light which shall be exhibited in sufficient time to prevent collision. A VESSEL UNDER OARS may exhibit the lights prescribed in this rule for sailing vessels, but if she does not, she shall have ready at hand AN ELECTRIC TORCH OR LIGHTED LANTERN showing a white light which shall be exhibited in sufficient time to prevent collision.*

e) *A VESSEL PROCEEDING UNDER SAIL (in daylight) WHEN ALSO BEING PROPELLED BY MACHINERY shall exhibit forward where it can best be seen A CONICAL SHAPE DOWNWARDS.*

This is rarely observed.

Rule 26 – Fishing vessels

a) A vessel engaged in fishing, whether under way or at anchor, shall exhibit only the lights and shapes prescribed in this rule.

Wishful thinking!

b) A VESSEL ENGAGED IN TRAWLING . . . shall exhibit:
   (i)   TWO ALL-ROUND LIGHTS in a vertical line, THE UPPER BEING GREEN AND THE OTHER WHITE, or (by day) a shape consisting of two cones with their apexes together in a vertical line one above the other;
   (ii)   A MASTHEAD LIGHT ABAFT OF AND HIGHER THAN THE ALL-ROUND GREEN LIGHT; a vessel of less than 50 metres in length shall not be obliged to exhibit such a light but may do so;
   (iii) when making way through the water, in addition to the lights prescribed in this paragraph, SIDELIGHTS and a STERNLIGHT.

Note that the single green all-round light is characteristic only of the trawler, although a dredger and a minesweeper may show two or three green lights respectively.

c) A VESSEL ENGAGED IN FISHING OTHER THAN TRAWLING shall exhibit:
   (i)   TWO ALL-ROUND LIGHTS in a vertical line, THE UPPER BEING RED AND

Fog

THE LOWER WHITE, or (by day) a shape consisting of two cones with apexes together in a line one above the other;

(ii) when there is OUTLYING GEAR extending more than 150 metres horizontally from the vessel, an ALL-ROUND WHITE LIGHT OR A CONE APEX UPWARDS IN THE DIRECTION OF THE GEAR;

(iii) WHEN MAKING WAY THROUGH THE WATER . . . SIDELIGHTS and a STERNLIGHT.

[Annex II prescribes extra light signals for trawlers: TWO VERTICAL WHITE LIGHTS when SHOOTING their nets, WHITE OVER RED when HAULING nets, and TWO VERTICAL REDS when NETS FAST on an obstruction; TRAWLERS FISHING IN PAIRS may direct SEARCHLIGHTS at each other. The Annex also prescribes signals for purse seiners: TWO VERTICAL YELLOW LIGHTS, FLASH-ING ALTERNATELY every second, but only when the vessel is hampered by her gear].

Rule 27 – Vessels not under command or restricted in their ability to manoeuvre

a) A VESSEL NOT UNDER COMMAND

(NUC for short)

shall exhibit:
(i) TWO ALL-ROUND RED LIGHTS in a vertical line where they can best be seen;
(ii) TWO BALLS (by day) or similar shapes in a vertical line where they can best be seen;
(iii) WHEN MAKING WAY through the water . . . SIDELIGHTS and a STERN LIGHT [in addition to two reds].

b) A VESSEL RESTRICTED IN HER ABILITY TO MANOEUVRE

(known as RAM),

except a vessel engaged in mine clearance operations, shall exhibit:
(i) THREE ALL-ROUND LIGHTS in a vertical line where they can best be seen; the HIGHEST AND LOWEST of these lights shall be RED and the MIDDLE light shall be WHITE;
(ii) THREE SHAPES

(by day)

in a vertical line where they can best be seen; the HIGHEST AND LOWEST of these shapes shall be BALLS and the MIDDLE one a DIAMOND;

9

(iii) WHEN MAKING WAY through the water, a MASTHEAD LIGHT or LIGHTS, SIDELIGHTS and a STERNLIGHT [in addition to three red/white/red];

(iv) when AT ANCHOR [in addition to red/white/red and shapes] the lights or shape prescribed in **Rule 30**

(ie at least one all-round white light forward, or one ball).

c) [A power-driven vessel hampered by towing should show a tug's lights and those of a vessel restricted in her ability to manoeuvre]

d) A VESSEL ENGAGED IN DREDGING or underwater operations, when restricted in her ability to manoeuvre, shall exhibit the lights and shapes prescribed in this rule and, in addition, when an obstruction exists:

'Coastguard on the radio wanting the name and address of your next of kin.'

(i) TWO ALL-ROUND RED LIGHTS OR TWO BALLS in a vertical line TO INDICATE the side on which the OBSTRUCTION exists;

(ii) TWO ALL-ROUND GREEN LIGHTS OR TWO DIAMONDS in a vertical line TO INDICATE the side on which another VESSEL MAY PASS;

(iii) [at anchor this rule still applies, not **Rule 30**]

e) Whenever the size of a VESSEL ENGAGED IN DIVING OPERATIONS makes it

Drizzle

impracticable to exhibit all lights and shapes prescribed in this rule, the following shall be exhibited:
- (i)   THREE ALL-ROUND LIGHTS in a vertical line where they can best be seen; the HIGHEST AND LOWEST of these lights shall be RED and the MIDDLE light shall be WHITE;
- (ii) a rigid replica of the INTERNATIONAL CODE FLAG 'A' not less than one metre in height.
f) A VESSEL ENGAGED IN MINE CLEARANCE OPERATIONS shall, in addition to the lights prescribed in Rules 23 and 30, exhibit THREE ALL-ROUND GREEN LIGHTS OR THREE BALLS; one of these lights or shapes shall be exhibited near the foremast head and one at each end of the fore yard. These lights or shapes indicate that it is DANGEROUS for another vessel TO APPROACH WITHIN 1000 METRES of the mine clearance vessel.
g) *[vessels of less than 12 metres need not comply with this rule unless engaged in diving operations]*

Rule 28 – Vessels constrained by their draught

A VESSEL CONSTRAINED BY HER DRAUGHT

CBD for short

may, in addition to the lights prescribed for power-driven vessels in Rule 23, exhibit where they can best be seen THREE ALL-ROUND RED LIGHTS in a vertical line OR A CYLINDER.

Signalling the 'Pecking Order

NUC	two vertical reds or two balls
RAM	three vertical red/white/red or ball/diamond/ball
CBD	three vertical reds or a cylinder
Fishing	green over white or red over white, or twin cones
Sailing	red over green or combined red and green
Power	white all-round or masthead white

Rule 29 – Pilot vessels

a) A VESSEL ENGAGED ON PILOTAGE DUTY shall exhibit:
- (i)   at or near the masthead, TWO ALL-ROUND LIGHTS in a vertical line, the UPPER BEING WHITE AND THE LOWER RED;
- (ii) WHEN UNDER WAY, in addition, SIDELIGHTS AND A STERNLIGHT;

(iii)   when at anchor, in addition to the lights prescribed in this rule, the lights or shape prescribed in **Rule 30** for vessels at anchor.

Rule 30 – Anchored vessels and vessels aground

a) A VESSEL AT ANCHOR shall exhibit where it can best be seen:
   (i)   IN THE FORE PART, an ALL-ROUND WHITE LIGHT OR ONE BALL;
   (ii)   at or NEAR THE STERN AND AT A LOWER LEVEL than the light prescribed in sub-paragraph (i), an ALL-ROUND WHITE LIGHT.
b) A VESSEL OF LESS THAN 50 METRES in length may exhibit an ALL-ROUND WHITE LIGHT WHERE IT CAN BEST BE SEEN instead of the lights prescribed in paragraph a) of this rule.
c) A vessel at anchor may, and A VESSEL OF 100 METRES AND MORE in length SHALL, ALSO USE THE AVAILABLE WORKING OR EQUIVALENT LIGHTS to illuminate her decks.
d) A VESSEL AGROUND shall exhibit the lights prescribed in paragraph a) or b) of this rule and IN ADDITION, where they can best be seen:
   (i)   TWO ALL-ROUND RED LIGHTS in a vertical line;
   (ii)   THREE BALLS in a vertical line.
e) *A VESSEL OF LESS THAN 7 METRES in length, when AT ANCHOR NOT IN OR NEAR A NARROW CHANNEL, FAIRWAY OR ANCHORAGE, or where other vessels normally navigate, SHALL NOT BE REQUIRED [to comply with this rule].*
f) *A VESSEL OF LESS THAN 12 METRES in length, WHEN AGROUND SHALL NOT BE REQUIRED [to comply with this rule].*

In spite of the immense care taken in drafting the colregs, the lights prescribed in Rules 20 to 30 can occasionally be ambiguous, and when at sea they can often be confusing.

To take the simplest example – a single white light: for exam purposes it could be several things (sternlight, anchor light, small powerboat under way); at sea, the context might resolve the ambiguity (a power boat will move, whereas an anchor light will not); but if the observer is also confronted by an array of shorelights, the single white might simply go unnoticed.

Because the surrounding darkness deprives you of other references, distant shore lights can temporarily be mistaken for a mysterious – nonexistent – vessel close to. And certain types of ship are notoriously confusing – warships, fishing vessels, ferries, or any other vessel whose decks are ablaze with working lights. By contrast, the twin masthead lights and sidelights of a darkened ship are remarkably effective in conveying her relative movement.

Dangerous underwater wreck

PART D – Sound and light signals

Rule 32 – Definitions

b) ['short blast' means about 1 second]
c) ['prolonged blast' means 4–6 seconds]

Rule 33 – Equipment for sound signals

a) A VESSEL OF 12 METRES OR MORE in length shall be provided with a WHIS-TLE AND A BELL, and a VESSEL OF 100 METRES OR MORE in length shall, IN ADDITION, be provided with a GONG, the tone and sound of which cannot be confused with that of the bell.
b) *A VESSEL OF LESS THAN 12 METRES in length shall NOT be OBLIGED TO CARRY the SOUND SIGNALLING APPLIANCES PRESCRIBED in this rule, but IF SHE DOES NOT, she shall be provided with SOME OTHER MEANS of making an efficient sound signal.*

Rule 34 – Manoeuvring and warning signals

a) When vessels are in sight of one another, a POWER-DRIVEN VESSEL UNDER WAY, when manoeuvring as authorised or required by these rules, shall indicate that manoeuvre by the following signals on her whistle: ONE SHORT BLAST – 'I AM ALTERING MY COURSE TO STARBOARD'
TWO SHORT BLASTS – 'I AM ALTERING MY COURSE TO PORT'
THREE SHORT BLASTS – 'I AM OPERATING ASTERN PROPULSION'
b) ANY VESSEL MAY SUPPLEMENT the WHISTLE SIGNALS prescribed in this rule BY LIGHT SIGNALS:
ONE FLASH – 'I AM ALTERING MY COURSE TO STARBOARD'
TWO FLASHES – 'I AM ALTERING MY COURSE TO PORT'
THREE FLASHES – 'I AM OPERATING ASTERN PROPULSION'
[ie 1-second flashes, and 10 seconds between signals; signalling light is white, all-round, visible at minimum of 5 miles]
c) When in sight of one another in a narrow channel or fairway:
  (i)   a VESSEL INTENDING TO OVERTAKE another shall in compliance with **Rule 9e (i)** indicate her intention by the following signals on her whistle:
TWO PROLONGED BLASTS FOLLOWED BY ONE SHORT – 'I INTEND TO OVERTAKE YOU ON YOUR STARBOARD SIDE'
TWO PROLONGED BLASTS FOLLOWED BY TWO SHORT – 'I INTEND TO OVERTAKE YOU ON YOUR PORT SIDE'
  (ii)   the VESSEL ABOUT TO BE OVERTAKEN when acting in accordance with **Rule 9e (i)**
shall INDICATE AGREEMENT by the following signal on her whistle:
ONE PROLONGED, ONE SHORT, ONE PROLONGED AND ONE SHORT BLAST

'I can't find what "continuous short blasts" means in the almanac.'

d) When vessels in sight of one another are approaching each other and from any cause either VESSEL FAILS TO UNDERSTAND THE INTENTIONS OR ACTIONS of the other, OR IS IN DOUBT WHETHER SUFFICIENT ACTION IS BEING TAKEN by the other TO AVOID COLLISION, the vessel in doubt shall immediately indicate such doubt by giving at least FIVE SHORT AND RAPID BLASTS on the whistle. Such signal may be supplemented by a light signal of at least five short and rapid flashes.

e) A VESSEL NEARING A BEND or an area of a channel or fairway where other vessels may be obscured by an intervening obstruction shall sound ONE PROLONGED BLAST. Such signal shall be ANSWERED WITH A PROLONGED BLAST by any approaching vessel that may be within hearing around the bend or behind the intervening obstruction.

Rule 35 – Sound signals in restricted visibility

In or near an area of restricted visibility, whether by day or night:

a) A POWER-DRIVEN VESSEL MAKING WAY THROUGH THE WATER shall sound, at intervals of not more than 2 minutes, ONE PROLONGED BLAST.

Visitors' moorings

b) A POWER-DRIVEN VESSEL UNDER WAY BUT STOPPED and making no way through the water shall sound, at intervals of not more than 2 minutes, TWO PROLONGED BLASTS in succession with an interval of about 2 seconds between them.

c) A vessel NOT UNDER COMMAND, a vessel RESTRICTED IN HER ABILITY TO MANOEUVRE, a vessel CONSTRAINED BY HER DRAUGHT, *a SAILING vessel*, a vessel ENGAGED IN FISHING and a vessel ENGAGED IN TOWING OR PUSHING another vessel shall, instead of the signals prescribed in paragraphs a) or b) of this rule, sound at intervals of not more than 2 minutes, three blasts in succession, namely ONE PROLONGED FOLLOWED BY TWO SHORT BLASTS.

d) A vessel engaged in fishing when at anchor, and a vessel restricted in her ability to manoeuvre when carrying out her work, shall instead of the signals prescribed in paragraph g) of this rule, sound the signal prescribed in paragraph c) of this rule.

e) A VESSEL TOWED or if more than one vessel is towed the last vessel of the tow, if manned, shall at intervals of not more than 2 minutes sound four blasts in succession, namely ONE PROLONGED FOLLOWED BY THREE SHORT BLASTS.

f) [pushing tug and pushed vessel if rigidly connected are regarded as single power-driven vessel]

g) A VESSEL AT ANCHOR shall AT INTERVALS OF NOT MORE THAN ONE MINUTE RING THE BELL RAPIDLY for about 5 seconds. In a VESSEL OF 100 METRES OR MORE in length the BELL SHALL BE SOUNDED IN THE FORE PART of the vessel AND IMMEDIATELY AFTER the ringing of the bell the GONG shall be SOUNDED RAPIDLY for about 5 seconds IN THE AFTER PART of the vessel. A vessel at anchor MAY IN ADDITION sound three blasts in succession, namely ONE SHORT, ONE PROLONGED AND ONE SHORT BLAST, to give warning of her position and of the possibility of collision to an approaching vessel.

h) A VESSEL AGROUND shall give the bell signal and if required the gong signal prescribed, and IN ADDITION, give THREE SEPARATE AND DISTINCT STROKES ON THE BELL IMMEDIATELY BEFORE AND AFTER THE RAPID RINGING of the bell. A vessel aground may in addition sound an appropriate whistle signal.

i) *A VESSEL OF LESS THAN 12 METRES in length shall NOT be OBLIGED TO GIVE the ABOVE-MENTIONED SIGNALS but if she does not, shall make some other efficient sound signal at intervals of not more than 2 minutes.*

j) A PILOT VESSEL when engaged on pilotage duty MAY IN ADDITION to the signals prescribed in this rule sound AN IDENTITY SIGNAL OF FOUR SHORT BLASTS.

2 vertical red lights

Communications

Maritime communications have evolved over hundreds of years, from the signal flags to which Nelson turned a blind eye, through semaphore, Morse telegraphy and the Aldis lamp, to various forms of voice radio. Current systems make extensive use of satellites and – mostly importantly for yachtsmen – VHF (Very High Frequency) radiotelephones.

But elements of the older systems remain, and are still useful in certain situations. For example, the Morse code SOS (...---...) is still a universally recognised signal of distress; and the custom of flying a national courtesy flag at the crosstrees when visiting a foreign port is still much appreciated.

The would-be Yachtmaster is therefore expected to understand the principles of signalling by flags and Morse, and to have a working knowledge of VHF radio procedures. Students who go on to take the practical Yachtmaster Offshore exam must hold a radio operator's certificate.

Flags

Each letter of the alphabet is represented by one of the **international code flags**, which also have 'single flag meanings'. For instance, the blue and white flag for the letter 'P' – the 'Blue Peter' – is traditionally flown by a vessel about to set sail (it may also be familiar from racing start lines). On returning from a foreign port outside the EC you must fly the plain yellow 'Q' flag, to tell Customs that: 'My vessel is healthy and I request free pratique'.

Other flags that may be worth remembering are: 'A' – 'I have a diver down'; 'B' – 'I am taking in, or discharging, or carrying, dangerous goods' (it might be flown by a tanker or a naval auxiliary); 'W' – 'I require medical assistance'.

Apart from their use in signalling, flags provide a colourful link between today's yachting and the long traditions of the Royal Navy and the Merchant Marine. The four that mainly concern yachtsmen are the **ensign**, the **courtesy flag**, the **burgee**, and the **racing flag**.

The ensign is a maritime version of the national flag, flown at the stern. British yachts, like merchant vessels, fly the red ensign. Royal Navy ships and members of the Royal Yacht Squadron fly the white ensign. Some other yacht clubs have an ensign warrant entitling members to fly a blue ensign – normally used only by government departments. When passing a warship of any nationality it is customary to 'dip' your ensign, but this gesture should be used sparingly unless you are prepared to be snubbed by not necessarily having it returned! When visiting a foreign port, in addition to your own ensign, the ensign of the country you are entering should be flown, as a courtesy, at the starboard crosstrees.

The burgee is a triangular flag worn at the mainmast head to indicate wind direction and, by its design, membership of a particular yacht club. A simple

Vessel not under command

'He's flying "K" Sir – I wish to communicate with you!'

rectangular flag is sometimes flown instead of a burgee to show that a yacht is racing – and that her crew would appreciate being left to manoeuvre clear in a clean wind.

Morse code

Each flag in the international code of signals is also of course represented by a Morse symbol consisting of dots and dashes, conveyed by telegraphic buzzer or flashing lamp. The number of sailors who can communicate in this way is dwindling fast but, as is the case with flags, there are some Morse symbols, such as ...- ,'V' for Victory or Beethoven's fifth symphony, which are part of our permanent heritage. In a maritime context, it means 'I require assistance'. Apart from the dots and dashes of the composite SOS signal, and .--for 'W', as above, you might like to memorise ..- for 'U', meaning 'You are standing into danger'. Note also that the single blast on a ship's whistle, which tells other vessels that 'I am directing my course to starboard', has a Morse equivalent in the single flash of the letter 'E'. Two flashes, for 'I', means 'I am directing my course to port'.

VHF radio

The point about **VHF (Very High Frequency)**, as opposed to MF (Medium Frequency), radio is that it is virtually limited to 'line-of-sight' ranges – say about 10 miles from one yacht to another, or perhaps 30–40 miles when talking to a coastal radio station like the Coastguard. This limitation gives the paradoxical advantage that a lot of scattered craft can use the same frequency without getting in one another's way. Once in contact, VHF reception is likely to be clear; the equipment is relatively cheap; and the drain on your batteries is small. Indeed, modern technology even enables yachtsmen to use a waterproof **handheld VHF** set with its own batteries and aerial – like a mobile phone – provided they accept a much shorter range of operation than the conventional set with more power and a mast-mounted aerial.

Radio channels

A band of VHF frequencies is allocated under an international agreement for use by ships and yachts, divided into a large number of 'channels', or specific frequencies. Each channel is in turn allocated to a specific function – distress calls, intership calls, port operations, and so on.

For example, **Channel 16** is both the VHF international distress frequency and the calling channel on which most other calls are briefly initiated, before switching to a working channel so as to leave it clear for other traffic. Channel 16 is therefore essential on even the smallest maritime set. This is also true of Channel 6, the main intership working channel. The Coastguard use Channel 67, among others (see distress procedures), for communicating with small craft. Marinas in the UK often use Channel 80.

If the initial call is on Channel 16, then whoever answers will usually tell the caller to switch immediately to a specified working channel. In any event, **the maximum length of a non-distress call on Channel 16 is one minute**.

Using the same aerial to transmit and receive means that you cannot speak and listen at the same time. In other words, basic sets are limited to 'simplex' operation, in which each transmission ends with the characteristic word 'over' to invite the other person to speak (although some sets are designed for 'duplex' conversation on working channels intended for this purpose).

Basic procedures in radio communication

All radio operators develop their own jargon and procedures in order to speed up communication and avoid any possible ambiguities. The marine fraternity are no exception; and although it may sound rather artificial at first – spelling with the phonetic alphabet, repeating key words with the introductory phrase 'I say again', turning 'a hundred and fifty' into 'one, five, zero', and so on – it has evolved from long practical experience.

The **basic procedure** is first to listen (to make sure you are not interrupting another call – especially a distress call), then identify the station or vessel you are calling, followed by your own identification, repeated, before inviting a

Occulting light (Oc) – light periods exceed dark

reply: eg 'THAMES COASTGUARD – THIS IS YACHT SO AND SO, YACHT SO AND SO – OVER', to which the answer might be: 'Yacht SO AND SO – THIS IS THAMES COASTGUARD – CHANNEL 67 – OVER'.

The full procedure can be found in the RYA pamphlet G22, to which your instructor will no doubt refer you – especially if you are going on to take the practical Yachtmaster exam, for which, as we have already said, a radio operator's certificate is a prior requirement. But the main principles – such as not blocking Channel 16, keeping messages brief, formal and clear, and allowing a coastal radio station to control vital communications because of its longer effective range – are common sense.

The Phonetic Alphabet

A – Alpha	B – Bravo	C – Charlie
D – Delta	E – Echo	F – Foxtrot
G – Golf	H – Hotel	I – India
J – Juliet	K – Kilo	L – Lima
M – Mike	N – November	O – Oscar
P – Papa	Q – Quebec	R – Romeo
S – Sierra	T – Tango	U – Uniform
V – Victor	W – Whiskey	X – X-ray
Y – Yankee	Z – Zulu	

Distress signals

This is another area where electronic technology and automated procedures are gradually taking over, but have not yet replaced traditional methods.

A **VHF radio distress or 'Mayday' call** (from the French *m'aidez*) should only be made when you or your yacht are in 'grave and imminent danger' and require 'immediate assistance'. The standard procedure is as follows:
Select Channel 16 at high power and speaking slowly and clearly, transmit:

- 'MAYDAY, MAYDAY, MAYDAY' –
- 'THIS IS (name of yacht, repeated three times)' –
- 'MAYDAY (name of yacht, spoken once)' –
- 'MY POSITION IS (lat. and long., or true bearing and distance from charted mark)' –
- 'I AM (sinking, on fire, or whatever)' –

- 'I HAVE (number of persons on board who are eg taking to a liferaft and/or firing distress rockets)' –
- 'I REQUIRE IMMEDIATE ASSISTANCE' –
- 'OVER'

Transmitting signals automatically

Since the introduction of the **Global Maritime Distress and Safety System (GMDSS)**, you can transmit the first part of this call (that is, the Mayday, the yacht's identity, and position) automatically, using a digital attachment to your VHF set. The attachment is known as a **Digital Selective Calling (DSC)** controller, which operates on Channel 70.

Each controller is programmed with a unique nine-digit number – the **Maritime Mobile Service Identity (MMSI) number** – which acts rather like a telephone number, rather than a name, to identify the vessel that carries it. A Coastguard station receiving an automatic distress call therefore knows who is in trouble, and if the DSC controller is linked to a GPS unit – as the GMDSS assumes – the station also receives that vessel's position (alternatively, the controller can be manually programmed with the latest position and its time). The person needing assistance waits 15 seconds for an automatic acknowledgment from the Coastguard, or a DSC-equipped ship, before repeating the distress call by voice on Channel 16, giving his or her MMSI number as well as the vessel's name or callsign.

The type of controller designed for small craft cannot automatically acknowledge a DSC distress call it receives, so it is more than usually important for a yacht in this situation to wait a while before intervening. It is vital that the rescue services, with their powerful communications, should take control as soon as possible. However, when it is clear that a distress call in any form has not been heard elsewhere, the message should be '**relayed**' (that is, passed on) on Channel 16, preceded by the words 'MAYDAY RELAY, MAYDAY RELAY, MAYDAY RELAY'.

The **GMDSS** is a complicated system that will take time to settle down, and may well be modified along the way. For the foreseeable future, it will be **compulsory only for merchant ships of more than 300 gross tons,** and certain fishing vessels. So although the IMO assumes that eventually leisure craft will also be DSC-equipped, yachtsmen can continue to use the basic VHF system. The crucial change in that respect is that **from February 2005, the Coastguard will cease to maintain a dedicated 'headset' distress watch on Channel 16** – although they will still be monitoring this channel as a supplement to the automatic system and for other communications.

Another type of automatic distress signal under the GMDSS umbrella is provided by an **Emergency Position Indicating Radio Beacon (EPIRB);** this uses satellites to alert the rescue services.

Special mark

However, there are many situations falling short of 'grave and imminent danger' when help is nevertheless urgently needed, or nearby shipping needs to be informed. A yacht might be dismasted and struggling to sort out the damage, or drifting across a shipping lane with a fouled propeller. Or there might be a serious medical emergency on board. In such cases, an **'urgency' radio signal** to 'ALL STATIONS' should be made, preceded by the words 'PAN-PAN, PAN-PAN, PAN-PAN', giving the yacht's name and position, followed by a brief explanation of the problem. A call specifically seeking medical advice may be preceded by the words 'PAN-PAN MEDICO', repeated three times.

Other ways of calling for assistance

If GMDSS is at one end of the spectrum of internationally recognised distress signals, then 'flames on the vessel' is probably at the other. The means usually suggested for making this ancient signal is a burning tar barrel – something few of today's yachts carry! However, there are many **other ways of calling for assistance**:

- Red hand flare or rocket
- Orange smoke flare
- SOS Morse signal by any means
- International code letter V, by Morse or flag – 'I require assistance'
- International code flags NC
- Square flag with a ball over or under it
- Continuous sounding of a fog horn
- Continuous raising and lowering of the arms

Maritime and Coastguard Agency

If you ever have to use the distress signals, it will probably be the Coastguard that sends a lifeboat or a helicopter to your rescue. The service was founded in 1822 to prevent smuggling, but nowadays it operates through a network of **coastal rescue centres**, manned 24 hours a day – six main Maritime Rescue Co-ordination Centres (Aberdeen, Yarmouth, Dover, Falmouth, Swansea and Clyde), and 15 Sub-Centres. With their powerful VHF and MF (150-mile range) radio communications, these centres are at the heart of the GMDSS.

But with the demise of commercial coastal radio stations in the UK, the Coastguard has taken on additional responsibilities. Navigation warnings have been added to its four-hourly schedule of **weather broadcasts** (inshore forecasts and gale warnings) and its co-ordination centres also arrange **medical link calls** to provide sailors with urgent medical advice.

Safety equipment

There is no absolute safety at sea, any more than on land, so any discussion of safety equipment and practice is a matter of personal judgement and compromise. But for exam purposes, err on the side of caution and whatever guidance your instructor offers. The standards listed below are based on RYA/DoT recommendations.

On one point there can be no argument: everyone on board should have some sort of **lifejacket**. A proper lifejacket, as opposed to a **buoyancy aid**, is designed to turn an unconscious person on to his back and support his head above water. However, the advantage of some buoyancy aids – those that double as oilskins or windproof waistcoats, for example – is that you are more likely to be wearing them when you fall overboard.

You will also need enough **safety harnesses** to equip the watch on deck in bad weather and at night. Small children need them anyway, and the DoT recommends one for each person on board. When choosing attachments points, avoid the size of U bolt that will neatly prize open a simple spring hook when pulled across it. For deck work in heavy weather, strong jackstays fore- and-aft are the best attachment.

A yacht should carry at least two **lifebuoys** for throwing to a man overboard (buoyant kapok-filled cushions also throw well) with a long floating line available if it is appropriate. At night, an **automatic light** attached to the lifebuoy (the light comes on when it inverts in a floating position) could be a lifesaver. Even during the day, keeping a continuous watch on the man overboard is one of the most vital aspects of the man-overboard drill – and made much easier if you can drop a tall **danbuoy** of the type that fishermen use to mark lobster pots.

Man overboard – abandoning ship

Should the worst happen, a **good technique for picking somebody up in the water** is to reach away (watching all the time), come about and reach back, staying slightly downwind so as to luff up to them, feathering the sails. Trailing a lifebuoy could retrieve the situation if you miss. Using the engine may be the answer, but in that case beware of lines round the prop. Once alongside, getting somebody back aboard (and they may well be suffering from exhaustion) will probably be much easier with a **boarding ladder**.

Offshore, a **liferaft** may be called for. But do *not* be tempted to abandon the yacht unless it is sinking fast or on fire – many crews have been lost in this

Tidal stream

way while their abandoned yacht has stayed afloat and been recovered. The exception to this rule is a situation where a **rescue helicopter** instructs you to take to the water – in a lifejacket, a dinghy, or a liferaft, at the end of a long warp – so as to make winching you up easier. The winching wire will be preceded by a light line to guide it down (let the wire touch the water before handling it, to discharge static electricity). If a winchman comes down to take charge of the lift, he will probably land on the port quarter. Clear the decks, as far as possible, of anything that might snag the wire – and never make it fast. The lifting strop goes under your armpits, and tightens with a toggle. Then keep your arms down, even though this feels unnatural. If radio communication is possible, it will almost certainly be on Channel 16.

If you know a helicopter or a lifeboat is nearby and searching for you, the best way to direct it may be to use a **distress flare**. Offshore yachts should carry a mixed pack of flares – a minimum of four red parachute rockets (which can be seen from a great distance provided they are not fired into low cloud), four red hand flares, and two orange smoke signals (for high visibility by day). White flares are a valuable 'deterrent' to ships on a collision course at night that have apparently failed to see your navigation lights or your radar echo. A powerful **waterproof torch** should also be carried for this (and many other purposes). In fact, it does no harm to have two torches – one for everyday use, the other kept handy for real emergencies.

Fire and explosions on board

Fire can be more dangerous at sea than on land, even though one is surrounded by water. Any yacht with either an engine – especially a petrol engine – or cooking equipment needs at least one fire extinguisher. The recommended equipment for smaller yachts is two 1.5-kilogram dry powder **extinguishers** (carbon dioxide or foam are alternatives, but powder is what the fire brigade use for their own vehicles). They should be stored away from potential sources of fire, one at each end of the boat. Large motor yachts should have an automatic extinguisher built into the engine compartment.

A **fire blanket** is worth having to smother fires, for example in the galley. And of course sea water may be the answer, provided you are not dealing with spilt engine fuel. In any case, every boat needs at least one **bucket** on a lanyard, preferably two, and a flat bailer for the dinghy.

Far worse than a simple fire is the danger of exploding petrol fumes or cooking gas. This gas is heavier than air, so if it does escape it tends to collect in the bilges – which is why gas bottles should be stored in a separate locker that drains overboard. The most important single precaution is always to close the valve on the bottle when it is not needed. If there is a leak, a **gas detector** will provide warning. A diaphragm pump will help to clear the bilges.

Two **pumps**, which are easy to dismantle and can be worked from secure

'We were thinking of having a person-overboard drill, Joan.'

positions, are in any case a basic piece of safety equipment. It may be a good idea to make one of them an electric pump, which keeps going when you and your crew tire.

First aid kit

The boat's **first aid kit** should include seasickness tablets, dressings for burns, and painkillers. But perhaps the most important item is a book of first aid instructions, including mouth-to-mouth resuscitation and ways of treating hypothermia – because not knowing what to do for the best is sometimes the most frightening thing about an accident or injury. The *Macmillan Reeds Almanac* has a useful first aid section. In any case, a first aid certificate is a prior requirement of the practical Yachtmaster exam.

Radar reflectors and mobile phones

One piece of safety equipment that has become increasingly valuable as merchant ships get bigger and faster, and perhaps more careless of their small sisters, is a **radar reflector**, hoisted as high as possible. The basic type consists of aluminium plates slotted together in a shape known as an octahedral, and fixed so that it presents one of its hollow reflective corners to the radar transmitter's beam (and 'catches water' in the upper corner). More efficient for

South cardinal buoy

their size (that is, producing a bigger blip on the radar screen) are the kind of reflectors that encapsulate a number of hollow metal shapes in a plastic casing, which then hoists naturally in the correct position.

The humble **mobile phone** is sometimes scorned or ignored because it is very evidently not a substitute for a VHF marine radio. Yet within its limited range, it does offer another valuable way of contacting the emergency services ashore and has certainly saved lives. Don't mention it in the classroom, but do take your mobile phone aboard!

Safety equipment checklist

- Lifejackets – one for each crew member
- Safety harnesses – one for each crew member
- Lifebuoys – two
- Danbuoy
- Buoyant automatic light
- Boarding ladder
- Liferaft – inflated inflatable, or rigid dinghy with a lot of built-in buoyancy, are both viable options
- Flares – four red rockets, four red hand flares, two orange smokes, two white flares
- Fire extinguishers – two 1.5-kilogram ones
- Fire blanket
- Waterproof torch
- Radar reflector
- Foghorn
- Bilge pumps – two
- Bucket

Stability and buoyancy of yachts

Newly marketed yachts must nowadays demonstrate that they have the stability and buoyancy appropriate to their design category – 'A' (Ocean), 'B' (Offshore), 'C' (Inshore), or 'D' (Sheltered Waters). Conscious of this, the RYA publishes pamphlet G23, analysing the factors that affect these qualities. Apart from the special case of the catamaran, the main point to note is that adding equipment – particularly mast-mounted radar antennas and headsail furling gear – will reduce stability. Commonsense it may be, but this is a point still sometimes ignored.

Anchoring

Two anchors should be carried – a **main** bower, preferably with chain, and a smaller **kedge**, which is easier to handle and lay out from a dinghy. The catenary of a heavy chain helps to maintain the required horizontal pull on the anchor and prevent the boat sheering around. If warp is used for the main anchor it should be made of plaited nylon, and at least three fathoms of chain should in any case be attached to it at the anchor end.

The rule of thumb for anchoring with chain is to let out **at least four times the depth of water, and with warp at least six times.**

Types of anchor

The various **designs of anchor** are usually distinguished by their holding efficiency once they settle in (in soft ground the plough or CQR types hold much better, pound for pound, than the traditional fisherman), the way they stow (the fisherman and the Danforth stow flat), and their ability to cope with different kinds of seabed. The Bruce type – a relative newcomer – is awkward to stow on a flat deck, but has good holding power and no moving parts to trap fingers. Each design therefore has its advocates, but it is safe to generalise that a fisherman will cope better with kelp or seaweed, while a digging anchor is more suited to sand and mud, or a sandy bottom strewn with rocks.

Choosing an anchoring berth

When **choosing an anchoring berth,** first check the nature of the bottom, then calculate the depth of water that will be left at low tide (the Rule of Twelfths). Make sure you have room to swing when the tide changes. Finally, imagine the berth in the worst conditions you are likely to encounter before you leave. Would you have room to sail the anchor out at low water in a freshening onshore breeze?

A buoyed **tripping line** from the head of your anchor may be advisable when you know the ground is foul with old chain, but is often more trouble than it is worth.

Coping with bad weather

The most obvious kind of bad weather is a gale, but in a shipping lane like the Dover Strait, half choked with sandbanks and a ship passing every five minutes, **fog** can be just as much of a hazard – especially since sea fog can coexist with a fresh breeze that in itself brings problems for small sailing craft. At least the wind brings manoeuvrability, removing that sense of helplessness that comes with lying becalmed in poor visibility. If there are ships about in these

I require medical assistance

conditions, it is a fine point of judgement as to when to switch on an auxiliary engine – thereby exchanging the ability to hear danger approaching, for the speed to get out of the way if it actually arrives. In any case, the engine should be warmed up and ready for instant use.

Commonsense precautions in fog include plotting the most accurate possible position before it clamps down (this is when the methodical navigator scores), wearing lifejackets, having a dinghy towing or ready to launch, and using a foghorn (though on a big ship's bridge it will not be heard in time to make any difference). In many situations the safest course will be to sound your way into shallow water where large vessels cannot follow, or at least keep clear of obvious shipping lanes.

Fog precautions

- Plot position at first sign of worsening visibility
- Maintain plot, eg with GPS
- Hoist radar reflector if not permanently rigged
- Put on lifejackets
- Launch (or at least prepare) dinghy
- Increase look-out and, if under power, stop engine periodically to listen
- Sound foghorn every two minutes
- Consider sounding into shallow water

The key to **surviving strong winds** in relative comfort and safety is anticipation, starting with your Yachtmaster's weather forecasting skills and a basic decision as to whether to run for shelter or find some sea room to ride it out – a choice that even lifeboatmen have sometimes got wrong.

In rough weather, especially if you cannot heave-to, almost everything is much more difficult and tiring than usual, even just moving about or filling a kettle, and seasickness may make matters even worse. The aim, therefore, is to reduce to a minimum the number of things that will have to be done during a blow by thinking ahead and making preparations – putting on oilskins before you get wet; stowing loose gear securely; sealing hatches; getting out the safety harnesses; shortening sail early (before you really need to, unless of course you are racing); preparing some simple food; looking up navigational data you may need; planning where you will bolt if an unexpected gear failure forces you to run off downwind, and so on. If night is coming on, all this still applies only *more* so.

$\longrightarrow$

Heavy weather checklist

- Secure loose gear on deck and below
- Put on lifejackets and safety harnesses
- Rig jackstays if not permanent
- Put in reef or reefs (maybe one more than you immediately need)
- Take seasickness tablets if required
- Prepare some simple food that's stored in accessible lockers
- Pre-plan navigation and escape routes

Passage planning

Getting out the charts to plan and anticipate a passage can be great fun (better than the real thing in some cases!) as well as saving time and trouble at sea.

Time can be saved, for example, by working your tides along a coastline; by setting out so that you arrive at a navigational corner like the North Foreland as the tide turns in your favour; by arranging coastal hops to avoid meeting the Portland race at full bore. If your destination is a river entrance with a tricky bar, you will make things easier for yourself if you arrive on the flood rather than the ebb, and the same obviously goes for shallow swatchways through the sands.

Going foreign, many navigators try to time their landfall for just before dawn, so as to make use of the lights to give an unmistakable fix, and then enter harbour in daylight.

As in preparing for a blow, anything done in advance, before leaving harbour, will probably be easier than at sea – sorting out charts, programming the GPS, looking up harbour entrance signals, noting the times of high water, plotting a couple of likely courses, and so on.

Planning a passage

- Small-scale chart – choose best route to avoid hazards, optimise tides and landfall
- Large-scale charts and harbour plans – for destination and possible diversions
- Note times of HW and LW; check tidal streams
- Note relevant waypoints, light characteristics, harbour signals, limiting depths, clearing lines
- Calculate fuel requirements
- Plot initial track

Position line

PEYTON

It's ironic – the same week you pass your Yachmaster.'

If you are going foreign, you must inform **Customs** (complete Part 1 of Form C1331) only if you are sailing directly to a port outside the EC. Returning from abroad, you need fly the yellow 'Q' flag (and deliver Part 2 of Form C1331) only if arriving directly from outside the EC (the Channel Islands are considered to be 'outside') or if you have goods to declare – such as animals.

The environment

People are becoming more and more concerned about protecting the environment, and this extends to the sea – and hence to yachtsmen. Four **basic principles** are endorsed by the RYA:

- **Garbage** – do not dump it at sea, but keep it to dispose of ashore
- **Oily wastes** – prevent any discharge of oil, fuel or similar harmful substances at sea
- **Sewage** – do not discharge a sea toilet close inshore
- **Toxic wastes** – keep toxic or damaging chemicals (such as antifouling) out of the sea

---

Well, that's it! We hope we have done our bit to help you with the Yachtmaster course. Good luck with those exams, and good sailing!

● ● ● ▬ ▬ ▬ ● ● ●

Index

Admiralty charts 4-5
Admiralty List of Lights and Fog Signals 25
Admiralty Tide Tables 16-18, 21, 22
anchoring 88
anticyclones 38, 44

back bearing s 29
bearings 31
  compass 11-13
Beaufort wind scale 46-7
buoyage 7-9
Buys Ballots Law 42-3

cardinal buoys 7-9
chart datum 16, 17
chart symbols 5-7
charts 3-7
chartwork 26-36
clearing lines 31
clouds 41-3
collision, risk of 57
Colregs 52-77
communications 78-81
compass bearings 11-13, 27, 29
compass, magnetic 10-13
convection 37
cross track function (XTE) 35
crossed wind rule 42
Cruising Association Handbook 25

dead reckoning 26, 33
depression 38, 39, 40, 43-4
depth sounding 13-14
deviation 11
dew point 38
dipping distance of a lighthouse 27, 28
distance off 27
distress signals 81-3

echo sounder 13-14
estimated position 26
explosions on board 85-6

fire on board 85-6
first aid kit 86
fix, obtaining a 27-9
flags 78-9
fog 45, 89
forecasts, weather 48-51

giving way 63
Global Positioning System (GPS) 3, 14-15, 27, 35

gnomonic projection 4
GPS 3, 14-15, 27
  cross track function (XTE) 35
ground track 26
  plotting 32-3

head-on situation 62-3
heavy weather 88-9
high pressure 38, 44
hyperbolic systems 15-16

IALA (International Association of Lighthouse Authorities) 7-9
instruments, chart 26
International Regulations for Preventing Collisions at Sea 52-77
IRPCS 52-77

katabatic winds 45
knots 13
land breezes 45
lateral buoys 7-9
lead line 13
leading marks 30-1
lee bowing 36
light characteristics 6, 9
lighthouses 7
  taking a bearing of 28
lights and shapes on vessels 66-74
line of soundings 27
local weather 44-6
log 13
log, ships 36
Loran-C 15-16

man overboard 84-5
Maritime and Coastguard Agency 83-4
Mercator's projection 3
morse code 79

nautical almanacs 16-17
neap tides 16, 17

observed position 26
occlusion 38, 40
overtaking 61-2

passage planning 90-1
pilot books 25
plotting a course 32-3
polar front 37
position line 26, 27

radar reflectors 86-7
radio channels 80
Rule of the Road 52-77
Rule of Twelfths 18-19
running fix 31

safety 52-87
safety equipment 84-7
sailing directions 25
sea breezes 44-5
secondary ports 13
shaping a course 33-6
shipping forecasts 48-51
sound and light signals 75-7
soundings, depth 13-14
spring tides 16, 17
squalls 45
stability and buoyancy of yachts 87
standard ports 18
symbols, chart 5-7
synoptic charts 38-9

terms, weather 37-41
tidal curves 17-18, 21, 22
tidal diamonds 23
tidal stream atlas 23-5
tidal streams 23-5, 26
tides 16-25
traffic separation schemes 59-60
transferred position 26, 31
transits 27, 30-31

units of depth 5

variation 11-13
vectors 33
vessels in restricted visibility, conduct of 65-66
VHF radio 79-80

warm front 38
warm sector 44
water track 26
weather 37-51
  information, sources of 48-51
  terms 37-41
  coping with bad 88-9
  local 44-5
wind patterns 40
wind shifts 39
winds 44, 45, 46-7

Yachtmaster Offshore Course 1-2